COMPLETE GUIDE TO HUNTING

Hunting Allies

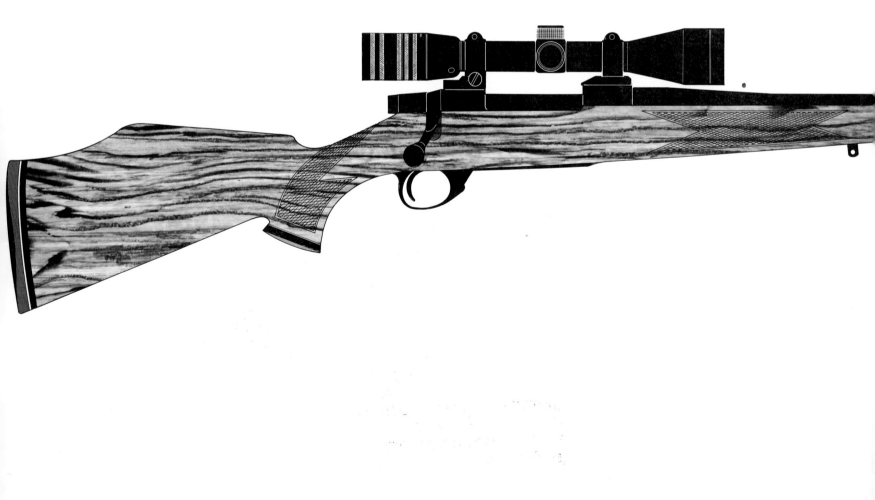

COMPLETE GUIDE TO HUNTING

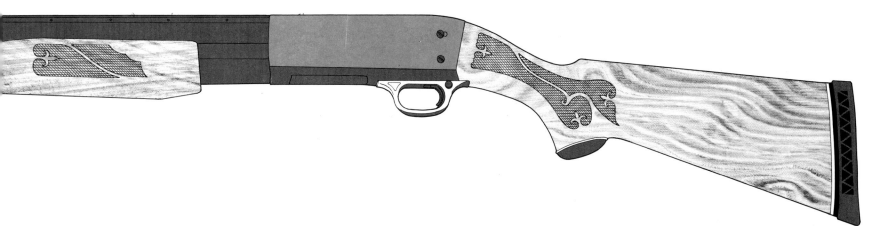

Hunting Allies

ROBERT ELMAN / *Supervising Editor*

MASON CREST PUBLISHERS, INC.

COMPLETE GUIDE
TO HUNTING

HUNTING ALLIES

This edition is published in 2002 by Mason Crest Publishers Inc.
370 Reed Road, Broomall, PA 19008, USA
(866) MCP-BOOK (toll free).
www.masoncrest.com

Editor-in-Chief: Robert Elman
Cover: Nordbok

First printing
1 2 3 4 5 6 7 8 9 10
Library of Congress Cataloging-in-Publication Data on file at the Library of Congress

ISBN 1-59084-502-1

Printed & bound in The Hashemite Kingdom of Jordan 2002

Supervising Editor

Robert Elman has participated in the project from its conception, and he has worked closely with the Publisher's editorial and art departments in guiding the authors, editing their material, and collecting the illustrations. Author of over a dozen books on hunting, he has hunted widely, and, as an editor, has specialized in books on hunting and outdoors.

Contents

I Hunting Allies

Chapter 1

The Hunting Dog

Nick Sisley

Dogs are important, and sometimes crucial, in both big- and small-game hunting, and they always have been. The hunting breeds are now separated into four basic categories, depending on what help the dog gives the hunter: retrieving, pointing, flushing, and chasing. While any hunting dog should be able to retrieve game, some species are specialists at doing this. The following selection of hunting dogs is not, of course, comprehensive, but nevertheless, it covers the important types used.

RETRIEVING DOGS

The three most important breeds are the labrador, the Chesapeake Bay retriever, and the golden retriever. The labrador is the most popular. Although technically spaniels, the American water spaniel and the Irish water spaniel are also retrieving dogs. All these breeds were developed for retrieving waterfowl, but the labrador and the golden retriever have, in recent decades, proved capable of flushing and retrieving game such as pheasant, grouse, woodcock, pigeon, rabbit, and others.

Labrador Retriever

The labrador is an ideal, all-round hunting dog and a perfect specialist for waterfowl retrieving. Hardy and tough, with a level of understanding rarely equaled by other breeds, a labrador can learn from a professional trainer, or from someone with less experience, although an amateur will take much longer to achieve the same results.

The most common color for a labrador is black, but they are also yellow and chocolate colored. They have a most friendly disposition, are particularly good around children, and are always ready to please the person who feeds them. Powerfully built, they usually weigh between 55 and 75 lb (25 to 34 kg). They have a relatively short but thick coat that keeps off the cold, and, as it is somewhat oily, it keeps the animal's skin dry even when it is swimming.

Labradors have an excellent record in field trials. The dogs were first imported in the nineteenth century to Britain from Newfoundland, having been brought there by Portuguese fishermen who had used them to retrieve fish and items of tackle (buoys, floats, net blocks, etc.) that were washed overboard during cod fishing. The name "labrador" has no connection with the Canadian territory that now bears that name but did not do so then. The word is simply the Portuguese for "worker" (i.e., working dog). The labrador's popularization in Britain is a subject on which there are conflicting versions, as the breed was already developed when imported into the country. The pioneers of labradors in Britain were, and still are, the Radclyffe family in Dorset.

Golden Retriever

This breed combines outstanding physical appearance with many qualities that make it a favorite among both waterfowlers and upland-game enthusiasts. While they are less hardy than labradors and Chesapeake Bay retrievers when fetching late-season waterfowl, golden retrievers are excellent for upland hunting. They take naturally to quartering and ranging fields, swales, and woods within easy gun range of their masters, and can flush and retrieve what is shot.

Generally weighing about 60 to 75 lb (27 to 34 kg), and standing over 20 inches (51 cm) at the withers, golden retrievers have longer hair than labradors. While their color is always golden, there can be a wide variation within this hue.

They are very affectionate animals and respond well to training that uses repetition, coaxing, and affection. Harsh methods are likely to produce a "cowed" retriever, but the breed's very ready affection can be almost a fault. The golden retriever is very popular with bench-show enthusiasts but, as yet, this has not had a detrimental effect on the breed.

It is generally accepted that the breed originated in 1865 in England, when a yellow dog named Nous was mated with a bitch of the now-extinct Tweed water-spaniel breed. Later, in the 1870s and 1880s, breeders introduced bloodhound and Irish setter blood into the breed, which was officially recognized by dog registries in England in 1910, in Canada in 1927, and in the United States in 1932.

Chesapeake Bay Retriever

About the same size as the other retrievers, the Chesapeake Bay has a unique coat: very thick, extremely oily, short with a slight curl, and with a woolly undercoat. No other breed's coat is so impervious to water. Its skin hangs loose on its body. Chesapeakes are brown, ranging from a dark shade to one that resembles dead grass. Unlike the friendly golden retriever, which usually wags its tail at an intruder, and the labrador, which usually barks, the Chesapeake will chase him off.

Not especially popular with field trialers, the Chesapeake is nonetheless highly favored by dedicated waterfowlers for, when called on to retrieve a bird from water half covered with thin ice, the dog plunges in when other breeds would be standing by shivering. However, the Chesapeake is not so good a dog on the uplands.

It is said that the breed had its beginnings when a dog and bitch swam ashore from a shipwreck off the Maryland coast in 1807. These two—Canton and Sailor—were, apparently, outstanding retrievers. The breed was developed through the latter part of the nineteenth century and was recognized by the American Kennel Club in 1933.

American Water Spaniel

This breed is smaller than the other retrievers, with a weight of between 25 and 40 lb (11 to 18 kg) and with a height of about 16 inches (41 cm) at the shoulder. Its color is a solid liver—dark, reddish brown—or chocolate, and its coat is compact and curly. Its tail is short and slender. It is easy to train, being biddable, easy to please, and also easy to care for (because it is relatively small). Its coat tends to pick up burrs and "stick-tights."

The American water spaniel was developed in the upper midwestern

A German shorthaired pointer puts
up a cock ring-necked pheasant and
the hunter steadies himself for a shot.

(Opposite) **GOLDEN RETRIEVER.**
The properly trained dog will sit still
as the hunter shoots and will move
only when given the order to fetch the
downed birds.
(Below) **LABRADOR.** This fine
retriever has just fetched a mallard
drake.

United States for use in small boats and canoes when hunting the lakes and marshes of the region. It is still much admired there, but less so elsewhere, although it deserves to be more popular with waterfowlers than it is. This is partly explained, perhaps, by the fact that the breed does not conform to the standards of beauty of the labrador and the golden retriever.

The breed is reputed to have descended from the old English water spaniels, with admixtures of Irish water spaniels and curly-coated retrievers, until the present breed took form. It was recognized by the American Kennel Club in 1940.

Irish Water Spaniel

This is a curly-coated breed that was developed in Ireland and first became popular in Britain and continental Europe before becoming widely accepted in North America because it could withstand tough, wintry conditions well. The breed generally weighs between 45 and 60 lb (20 and 29 kg) and has a solid liver color—dark reddish brown. The breed's popularity has fallen off, perhaps because shooting of waterfowl is now no longer unrestricted, and other breeds are better suited to a variety of uses.

As with many sporting breeds, the early history of this one is not definitely known but is believed to have started when Irish setters were crossed with French poodles.

Curly-coated and Flat-coated Retrievers

These breeds are similar in build—55 to 70 lb (25 to 32 kg)—and in coloring, being either black or liver, but they differ in temperament. The flat-coated tends to be a somewhat easy-going dog that is very biddable in marshes and uplands, and will flush and retrieve small game. It does well for a hunter who wants a close-working dog that seldom moves far from the gun.

Until the labrador "explosion" in the first decade of the twentieth century, the flat-coated retriever had been the dominant British gun-dog breed for thirty years. It supplanted the curly-coat in the 1880s after twenty years of curly dominance since the introduction of breechloading guns made driven game shooting possible, and thereby created the need for specialist retrievers. In muzzleloading days, all shooting was "rough," and pointers, setters, and spaniels did the retrieving, along with their other functions.

The curly-coated tends to be more spirited, and can flush and retrieve effectively. Only in New Zealand, however, have its qualities been fully recognized, for it is appreciated there as a superb water dog and is also popular among upland hunters. But both breeds deserve a higher standing than that which they are accorded.

POINTING DOGS

These breeds get their name from the way they respond to the immediate presence of the game they have located: they hold themselves rigid, pointing with their entire bodies towards the place where the game is concealed, waiting for a sign of command to flush it. Some point with a markedly upright stance, others in a lower crouching position. In order to find the game in the first place, pointers are trained to range systematically within gunshot, exploring each piece of cover in which birds or other game can be lying hidden.

They are invaluable in hunting game such as partridge, pheasant, woodcock, snipe, and quail, and any other game that characteristically does not fly up or run as soon as it detects danger.

They are naturally adept at finding wounded game that has gone to cover and at retrieving it. Like a retriever, a pointer will be considered "hard-mouthed" if it cannot carry an egg in its mouth without breaking it.

English Pointer

While the origins of this breed are both mixed and debated, it is generally regarded as the classic pointer, a rather aristocratic English dog, aloof where the setter, for example, is demonstratively affectionate. It is a short-haired breed, and generally white with markings or spots of liver, black, lemon, or yellow. It is trimly built and weighs between about 45 to 58 lb (20 to 26 kg).

One of the English pointer's most obvious characteristics is eagerness to hunt—occasionally to a fault. This can make a dog difficult to handle, as he is determined to find game, no matter where, and may range too far from the gun. However, a good trainer can curb this tendency to range too far. A well-trained dog is very staunch on point, steady to wing and shot, and almost tender in his manner of bringing to hand small birds such as quail. Occasionally, pointers are "hard-mouthed," but with training most of them can be excellent retrievers.

Very popular in the British Isles, the pointer is even more popular in North America. It is a favorite, for example, for ruffed-grouse shooting in the midwestern and northeastern United States, and it is used by pheasant hunters in many regions. Quail hunters in the southern states favor pointers when shooting in the immense grain fields, where the dogs will cast along the field edges while the hunters wait patiently in the center; when the pointer has picked up a scent, it will point until the hunters can move up and command the dog to flush the birds.

Some authorities hold that the breed originated in Spain at about the beginning of the seventeenth century, but dogs resembling pointers are to be seen in paintings from France from about the same period. The most generally accepted opinion is that the pointer evolved from a mixture of foxhound, greyhound, and bloodhound, crossed with the setting spaniels. As with much else characteristically British, the pointer developed its significant form in the middle and later nineteenth century, when the pioneering breeders—Thomas Statter, Sir Vincent Corbet, and J. Armstrong—contributed also to the development of the English, Irish, and Gordon setters.

When the world's first field trial was held, in England in the 1860s, pointers were not permitted to compete with setters, which were considered far superior, a position they held for a number of years, with the English setter holding first place. Eventually, the pointer came to the forefront and has maintained this position ever since.

In recent years, however, continental European breeds such as the German short-haired pointer and the Brittany spaniel have become relatively popular.

English Setter

A field-bred English setter stands about 21 to 26 inches (53 to 66 cm) high at the withers and weighs about 43 to 53 lb (19 to 24 kg). It is thus a little smaller than the pointer. The breed is basically white (making for a dog that can easily be seen in cover), with some ticking or spotting in one other color—black, blue, tan, lemon or orange, or liver. Some present-day breeders strive for dogs that are solid or nearly solid white. A setter with ticking but no real spotting is known as a belton, with a qualification to indicate coloring: most often blue belton. "Blue" here means a gray with a bluish sheen. The hair is fairly long, and the tail is beautifully "feathered."

A setter usually points in the manner of a pointer, that is to say, in the upright position of pointing head, uplifted front foot, and backward-pointing tail, but it will sometimes exhibit a trace of the crouching stance for which the breed's ancestors were noted some four centuries ago. John Caius, writing *Of Englishe Dogges* in 1570, remarked that when they detected scent strong enough to indicate that game was very close, they stopped and crouched—belly close to the ground—whereupon the huntsmen hurled nets over the concealed game. Setters possess a very strong inborn desire to hunt, and so are eager and hard-working, responding well to encouragement and repetition in training, and not to stern discipline. They point patiently and retrieve excellently.

Just when setters were first distinguished from other breeds is hard, if not impossible, to say with certainty, but it seems that they evolved from land spaniels, at least as early as the last quarter of the fourteenth century. Gaston de Foix, in *Le Livre de la Chasse*, from 1387, wrote of both land spaniels (springing, or flushing, spaniels of a sort used in falconry) and a type of setting spaniel. Later, some suggest, there were contributions to the breed from Spanish pointers, large water spaniels, and from springers.

Irish Setter

Even if this breed did not come from Ireland, its strikingly red coat and impulsive temperament would suggest its origins. It is slightly larger than the English setter but in recent years, bench-show tendencies have caused the breed to degenerate into a show type with little or no tractability, a complete lack of hunting sense, and an overall foolishness. A few breeders have counteracted this by breeding only from field-quality setters, and by infusing English setter blood from time to time in an effort to increase the animal's hunting instincts.

While there has been a revival of interest in the British Isles, a greater one has taken place in the United States, where the breed is registered with the American Field Dog Stud Book as "Red Setter," rather than Irish. It is popular, too, in many parts of continental Europe.

Gordon Setter

This is a black and tan setter of which only a few strains are being bred for the field at present, for their dark coloration has been a handicap in the field, while they—like the Irish setters—have become a victim of bench-show enthusiasm over superficial good looks. They might benefit from an infusion of English setter blood, for the typical Gordon setter tends now to be close-working and somewhat sluggish, if thorough, but can be trained to point well and to retrieve.

The breed derives from the southern English county of Sussex, where the Dukes of Richmond, whose family name is Gordon, are substantial landowners, and—once again in the nineteenth century—were responsible for the development, but not the inception, of this breed, for there is no question but that black and tan setters were trained and bred before then.

German Shorthaired Pointer

Weighing from about 50 to 70 lb (23 to 32 kg), the German shorthaired pointer is larger than the English pointer and raw-boned in comparison, although the breed is still developing fast, having become popular after World War II. Their tails are usually docked. Color is generally liver with some white ticking, although in many countries the breed has a great deal of white. This is claimed by some to be a result of unpublicized crosses with English pointers, made with the purpose of increasing the German dog's speed and willingness to range from the gun. Others consider it to be the result of selective breeding for color as well as good conformation and breeding.

However, the breed must still be considered a medium-ranging one, tractable and industrious, but without the pointing instinct of the English pointer or setter. In the hands of a good trainer, however, the German dog can develop this instinct well and become a staunch pointer.

The breed is an all-round one, a quality deriving from the general nature of its traditional work on the continent of Europe, where it has been used not only for birds but also for tracking and cornering boar, for bringing down deer if necessary, and even for killing cats and foxes on preserved ground. As a result, it is often too hard-mouthed to make a good retriever, but it can, as noted, be improved by good training.

Like most other breeds of hunting dog, this one has an ancestry that is undoubtedly ancient but equally undoubtedly obscure. Crosses between Spanish pointers and bloodhounds or Saint Hubert hounds, and later—in the nineteenth century—with English setters, produced a breed to which foxhounds and possibly setters had also contributed before a recognizable German shorthaired pointer emerged at the beginning of the twentieth century.

German Wirehaired Pointer (Drahthaar)

The longer of these two names for the same dog describes it the better, for its very coarse coat is wiry to the touch, and its face is whiskery. It is roughly the size of a large English setter, standing about 24 inches (61 cm) at the shoulder. Its color is predominantly liver, or liver with white ticking or small spots. Occasional examples are roan, an unusual color, but not unacceptable. The Drahthaar takes readily to waterfowl retrieving, but as it does not have the heavy coat of the labrador, golden, or Chesapeake Bay retriever, it is not recommended for retrieving in water in extremely cold weather. Its wiry hair does tend to dry quickly, however.

Most dogs of this breed are medium-ranging but tend to hunt out a little further than the average shorthair. They have excellent noses, are tough and resilient, and are eager to a fault to please their trainers or handlers, even to the point of becoming so attached that they forget what they are being trained to do; but this seldom happens in the field. They tend to be aloof with strangers.

The breed was developed in Germany by crosses between the griffon, the German shorthaired pointer, and the Pudelpointer.

Wirehaired Pointing Griffon

This breed is a solider version of the German wirehaired pointer, a slow-paced methodical worker for which grouse and woodcock are natural quarry; almost all other pointing dogs will beat him to coveys of quail and to pheasants. Its coat, while stiff and protective, has a much softer feel to it than those of other wirehaired dogs, and it is most commonly steel-gray or whitish-gray splotched with chestnut. Its tail is docked to about 6 inches (15 cm).

Griffons are easily handled, and are versatile, capable of pointing game, of trailing in the manner of a hound, and of retrieving from water. They are good in thick cover, where their coats protect them from briars.

The breed originated in Holland.

Brittany Spaniel

At 30 to 40 lb (14 to 18 kg), the Brittany spaniel is the smallest of the pointing dogs, but the only surviving pointing spaniel. It is extremely popular in France, Belgium, and Italy and has been increasing in popularity in the United States, but it does not have an established position in Britain, perhaps because of its French origins.

The typical Brittany has rather long legs on a compact body, giving it a slightly gangling appearance. Its coloration is normally white with orange, liver, or roan ticking or spots. The breed is usually soft in temperament, and it is best trained with coaxing and repetition. While they make fine family dogs, many remain aloof to affection, as do many dogs of pointing breeds.

They excel as retrievers and, with training, can learn to range out from the gun a little further than a medium distance. On game they can be trained to be very staunch, although they usually lack the intensity of point of typical pointers and English setters. They have become espe-

(Above) **ENGLISH SETTER**.
(Right) **GORDON SETTER**.
(Opposite) **GERMAN SHORT-HAIRED POINTER**.

16

cially popular with American hunters of ruffed (American) grouse and woodcock in the midwestern and northeastern United States and lower Canada. Brittany spaniels can make the switch to other game, such as snipe and waterfowl, but most make it less smoothly than the German shorthaired pointer, for example.

Vizsla

This is a Hungarian pointing dog—its name means "alert" or "responsive" in Hungarian—and about the size of a large pointer. It has a docked tail, weighs 50 to 60 lb (23 to 27 kg), is slim, and has a solid rusty-gold-colored coat. Its coat is short, making the breed unsuitable for work in thick cover, briars, or brambles but, with this exception, it is good at close work and at retrieving in the uplands. Vizslas seldom have the versatility to work marshes and other wetlands.

A few breeders have introduced some German wirehaired pointer or griffon blood into the breed, to remedy the thinness of its coat, while an enterprising kennel in the United States has taken to calling the breed the uplander, intending its dogs to be used for grouse and woodcock hunting.

Dogs strongly resembling modern vizslas were used by tenth-century Magyar falconers, and the developing breed was used by the Hungarian aristocracy in hunting on the plains, but in modern times, the breed has spread all over the bird-game hunting world.

Weimaraner

This breed is a large one: a big male can weigh almost 85 lb (38 kg) while standing no more than about 26 inches (66 cm) at the shoulder. The dogs have short, rather sparse hair, a tail that is usually docked, and blue-gray or pale amber eyes. The color of their coats is silver with mauve or taupe (gray with a brownish or other tinge) undertones when the light strikes it at a certain angle.

Like the vizsla, the Weimaraner is a dog for the uplands, where the breed works close, but without the tireless energy and eagerness of some pointing breeds. The Weimaraner's short hair renders it unsuitable for cold climates or frigid wet work.

The breed was developed in the mid-nineteenth century in Germany at Weimar, with the intention of producing an all-round performer in the hunting field and, although it has its loyal supporters, it is not among the most popular of breeds.

Two German wirehaired pointers on point and back. The dog in the foreground has located and pointed the birds, and the dog in the background is honoring the find by "backing."

FLUSHING DOGS (Spaniels)

These dogs work close to the hunter—once a falconer or hawker, now a shooter—quickly quartering the cover and finding a scent. As they do this, their tails wag faster and faster, thus signaling to the hunter that the appearance of game is imminent. When the scent becomes very strong, or when they see the quarry, they run in and bolt or flush it.

In England and on the continent of Europe, sportsmen expect a properly bred and trained spaniel to hunt furred and feathered game equally adroitly and eagerly. In North America, many prefer a spaniel to concentrate only on birds, evidently fearing that a bird dog that also bolts rabbits will lose his skill at putting up birds. This would be true of a pointing dog, for furred game behaves differently from feathered game when a dog approaches and points, and a pointer thus learns to specialize on the one or the other. But a flushing dog is not harmed by running a variety of game, and the hunter who restricts his spaniel to birds is denying his dog and himself an enjoyable and rewarding day's shooting. It is unfortunate that many American spaniel owners fail to understand this.

The word "spaniel" derives from the latinate name for Spain—Hispania—for dogs of a spaniel type were common there in the early medieval period, and spaniels of one kind or another evidently existed almost 2,000 years ago. By the mid-seventeenth century, several breeds were classified as either land or water spaniels, depending on their major talents, but since then, water spaniels have largely been replaced by the dogs classified as retrievers. The larger land spaniels are generally quite skillful at retrieving ducks. The most popular breed—the English springer spaniel—is accustomed, at many field trials, to display skill in making land and water retrieves, and to find, and flush or bolt, both winged and furred game.

While a number of other breeds have been equally impressive as the English springer, and are mentioned briefly here, only the English springer is described in detail. Chief among the other spaniels is the cocker, originally developed to flush woodcock. It is so handsome and small, and has so warm a personality that it become a great favorite of bench-shows and house-pet breeders. They bred it for the wrong qualities, lengthened its coat, weakened it, made it smaller, nervous and timid, and in the process lost its stamina, keen nose, and hunting desire, and so all but ruined it as a field dog. This was especially true in the United States.

Today, many people classify the English cocker spaniel as distinct from other cockers, and especially from the American bench-show type. It is more robust, if small by comparison with other bird dogs, and a fairly skillful and vigorous hunter. A few sportsmen still use it to hunt woodcock and even pheasant. It is good for hunting squirrels, too. It has not regained its former popularity, however, and good field strains are few.

Other spaniels of limited renown include the Clumber, the Sussex, and the Welsh springer spaniels. Even now, a Welsh springer that comes from field stock can be a good hunting dog, and it may be described as a slightly blocky, more stolid version of the English springer, so the hunter who wants a flushing dog is likely to choose the latter.

English Springer Spaniel

There are two distinct types of English springer spaniel: show and field. While they are registered as the same breed, they do not look alike, but it

is the field springer that has been, and is, the very best of the flushing spaniels from the hunter's point of view, and a hunter who wants a dog of this great breed must be careful to obtain one (or more) from field stock.

The field-bred springer is small as bird dogs go, is stockily built, standing typically less than 20 inches (50 cm) at the shoulder and weighing about 40 lb (18 kg) on average. Some are notably smaller. Those much larger are probably of show stock and should be avoided. The most common colors are white and liver, or white and black, with some ticking being typical, although not essential. The hair should be smooth to the touch, of a length similar to that of an English setter. There is some feathering at the back of the legs, and at the bottom of the docked tail. The ears are comparatively short, hanging not below the line of the jaw.

Perhaps the springer's most important quality is that it can be effective in the field with limited training. Merely being in "bird" country is usually enough for a dog to show he knows the fundamentals. Dogs of field-trial quality are another matter and must be trained with as much work and thoroughness as any other breed.

Springers tend to range naturally within gunshot and to quarter the territory effectively. They are also excellent retrievers, sometimes taking to it without training. Though their coat is relatively thin and does not permit water work in extremely cold conditions, they are excellent water dogs during moderate weather. A hunter who wants a dog for waterfowl should select one with a preponderance of black or liver, and a minimum of white, so that the dog will be less easily visible to wary ducks and geese. On the other hand, a whiter dog is easier for the hunter to see and keep track of in upland country.

Springers train readily, responding well to encouragement, and will cower before a strong verbal rebuke and seem confused if struck or treated harshly. They are perhaps the most affectionate and playful of all hunting dogs, and so make good family pets. In the field, the springer is the ideal pheasant dog and can also serve well on rabbits and hares, woodcock, snipe, partridge, and other game. While several breeds are known as utility dogs, this one is probably the most versatile all-purpose performer.

The breed was first accorded official classification in England in 1902. Springing spaniels had been known before then, as early as the sixteenth century, but there was no recorded attempt at developing a single uniform breed until much later. The Boughey family, of Aqualate, Shropshire, began carefully breeding dogs in 1812, and so established the first pure line of English springers.

The breed has been a very important one to shooters in the British Isles for many years. One of the most famous and successful breeding programs ever undertaken by a sportsman has been devoted to springers. Talbot Radcliffe, an English breeder, never sells a bitch, but his springer dogs have been exported and have established an international reputation for themselves, and for Talbot Radcliffe.

Many breeders in North America have also been extremely successful with springers, but it was not always so. Pointers and setters were much more popular at the turn of the century, for the most abundant game was the bobwhite quail and, in the Midwest, prairie chickens and sharp-tailed grouse; these were best coursed over the prairie and flushed by a pointer. It was the introduction of the ring-tailed pheasant, which prefers to sneak off or run from a point, that drew attention to the springer's skill at running in and flushing birds within range of their masters.

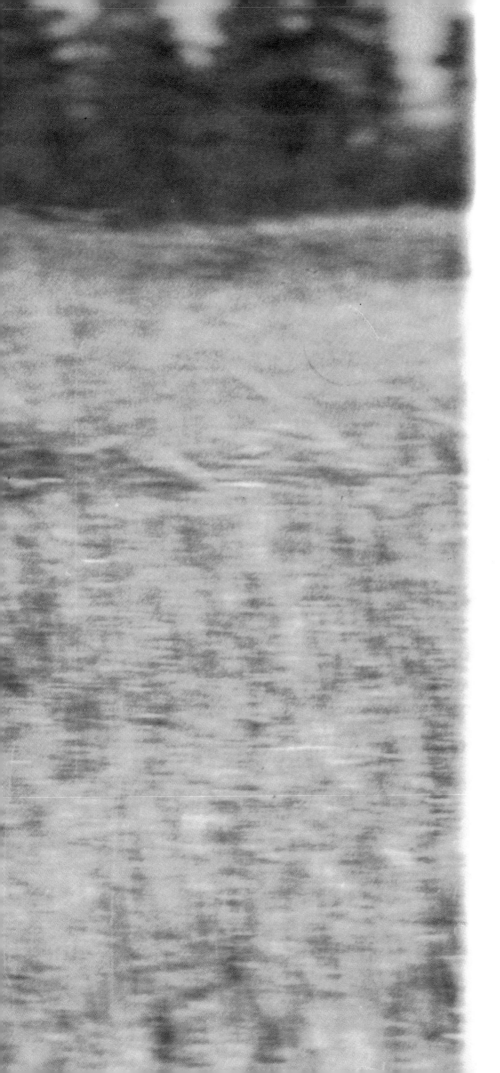

HOUNDS

Hounds are for the pursuit of game by scent, and while some are bred for speed—English foxhounds, for example—others run with endurance rather than great speed—beagles, for example, that are followed on foot in pursuit of hares. Most, however, follow the scent from the ground rather than from the air, as bird dogs do, and almost all give tongue when in pursuit: English foxhounds, Swedish elk-hunting *spetshund*, and American coon hounds are each of them unmistakable to their followers.

A great many breeds of hound still exist, although they are no longer used for hunting. The Afghan is perhaps the most ancient of them, and the bloodhound the best known (from detective fiction). Greyhounds and whippets, which hunt by sight, are still used extensively in Britain for coursing hare, while otterhounds—grey or grizzle rough-coated hounds—are now going to survive as show dogs, if at all, for otter-hunting is now illegal in Britain. Dachshunds are still occasionally used to bolt game rather than to pursue it. Other hounds include the Rhodesian ridgeback, the Irish wolfhound, the borzoi, the Scottish deerhound, the saluki, and the basenji, a hound that rarely barks.

Beagle

Beagles are the most popular hounds, both as pets and for hunting. For a hunting hound, the dog is not big, standing 13 to 15 inches (33 to 38 cm) at the shoulder. The typical coloration is a mixture of black, white, and tan. Beagles are short-coated, with long ears. Various explanations of the origin of the name sum them up: some consider "beagle" to derive from the Gaelic "beg," meaning small, others that it comes from the Old French "beegeule," meaning a noisy person, and the two together well describe a pack of beagles throwing tongue, as the expression is, on the scent of a hare, when they sound merry and musical, falling silent only when they lose the scent.

They work best in two or three couples or more, but single beagles will do well when hunting cottontail rabbits, snowshoe hares, or squirrels in North America. They will also flush pheasants, but they are fundamentally pack hounds, originating in Britain, where many organized packs of beagles exist, from the south of the country to the north.

Basset

Apart from the beagle, the basset is the only small hound of great importance to modern hunters. It is a short-legged, heavy-boned, large-bodied hound, standing about 12 to 15 inches (30 to 38 cm) at the shoulder, and most commonly has a color combination of black, white, and tan. Its ears are long and floppy, and its face, with its heavy flews, is solemn-looking.

Bassets are hare specialists and although slow—much slower than beagles—are keener-scented than any other pack hound and are exceedingly thorough, so that even if the hare outpaces them, it cannot hope to throw them off its track. A basset working alone will track a rabbit or squirrel and will flush a pheasant—but at its own deliberate pace. Bassets have deep, resonant voices.

The breed is of French origin, and is believed to have come about as the result of crossing the old French bloodhound with the small hounds of the Abbots of St. Hubert, a monastic order in Belgium several centuries ago. (St. Hubert is the patron of the hunt.) The breed developed in France, Belgium, and Russia, and in Britain in the late nineteenth century. The modern North American field strains have been bred from English and Russian stock and are somewhat trimmer than those of Britain.

English Foxhound

English foxhounds evolved into roughly their present form between two and three centuries ago, and have since then been bred for speed and stamina, largely within individual packs. In the 1920s and 1930s, Welsh foxhound blood was introduced into some English packs, to give an infusion of hardiness and scenting powers. A number of English packs, however, display marked individual characteristics, the hounds of the Belvoir Hunt, for example, being tan, a coloration noticeable in packs into which Belvoir hounds have been bred. In general, foxhounds are black, white, and tan, and stand about 21 to 25 inches (53 to 64 cm) at the shoulder. They are smooth-coated, have dropping ears, and carry their tails erect; their feet are hard-sinewed, making it possible to hunt twice a week in the season, and sometimes even more.

Their function is well known: to search an area where a fox is known or thought to be, and to force him into the open while, at the same time, communicating what they have found by "throwing their tongues"—a medley of sounds that the huntsman and experienced followers can interpret. Thereafter, the hounds pursue the fox across country, still "speaking to the fox" as they go, and they may cover 8 to 10 miles (13 to 16 km) in an hour.

American Foxhound

The history of the American foxhound can be traced to 1650, when the first European hounds were brought over. During the next couple of centuries, a good many more imported hounds—mostly English foxhounds not much different from those seen today—continued to be added to American stock. At the same time, there was considerable development of local strains throughout rural America. Families or geographic areas developed their own strains, and in many instances these dogs were used to pursue animals other than, or in addition to, the red and gray foxes. The most important additional game has included the raccoon, bobcat, bear, boar, cougar, and coyote.

Some authorities claim that no breed can match the American foxhound in the qualities needed for successfully trailing both the fox and other assorted game. Such a hound must have exceptional scenting ability, speed, stamina, a good voice, intelligence, a strong homing ability, proficiency at negotiating difficult terrain and ground cover, aggressiveness, and an eagerness to run the quarry either alone or with a pack. Some of the hunters who use hounds are careful to cast their animals only after a single species of game, and a dog of this type must be thoroughly trainable, so that he will not be distracted by the wrong quarry. Yet American foxhounds (and other American breeds) also have the inherent instincts that will permit them to be trained for hunting a variety of game.

Like the English foxhound, the American is usually tricolored—white, black, and tan—but orange, lemon, and other shades are often seen. The coat is short and dense, the average shoulder height 24 inches (61 cm), the average weight 50 to 60 lb (23 to 27 kg).

Of the many strains of American foxhounds, three have become most famous: the Walker, the Trigg, and the July. The Walker hound has now been developed into a separate, registered breed, while the other two are still registered as American foxhounds.

Walker Hound

The Walker hound is named for John Walker, a Virginia settler who moved to Kentucky and, primarily together with a fellow foxhunter, George Washington Maupin, bred this now distinct breed. Those hounds that showed ability to tree raccoons were bred further for this sport, and Walker hounds are now well known to raccoon hunters.

Both types of Walker are the same size, having an average shoulder height of about 24 inches (61 cm) and a weight of 50 to 70 lb (23 to 32 kg). Most are tricolored in black, white, and tan, and variations occur and are permissible for registration.

The breed was enhanced by a famous foxhound from Tennessee—Tennessee Lead—and has also English foxhound blood, in addition to infusions from the finest dogs of various strains from the surrounding region.

Today's Walkers are wide-ranging, relentless hunters with great speed, endurance, and homing instinct. One of their abilities, which contributes to their speed, is to take scent both from the air and from the ground.

American Coon Hound (Utility Hound)

This is a general name for a number of breeds of large hound that are mainly, but not exclusively, used to hunt raccoons. Packs of these hounds are also used to hunt foxes, as well as bear, boar, cougar, and bobcat (American lynx). In some regions, a hunter or guide may refer to his pack not as coon hounds but as bear hounds, boar hounds, or cat hounds, depending on their specialty. And depending on the region, the hunter, the available game, and the dogs themselves, they may be used to trail only one kind of game, or more—perhaps, for example, both bear and bobcat, or bear and boar.

In some regions, hound owners are unusually permissive with regard to cross-breeding, especially if the hounds are not registered. The owners are far more interested in trailing and treeing performance than in breed coloration or conformation. Such a pragmatic approach would not commend itself to the owner of a good English pointer bitch, if he were offered the services of an equally good Brittany spaniel.

The packs used for larger, dangerous game, such as bear or boar, must be fearless and tough, capable of keeping their quarry at bay by circling it and by repeatedly attacking and retreating. Naturally enough, hounds are sometimes injured or killed in this way. A cougar may be reluctant to come down from a tree or a ledge where it may have been cornered, but when it does, it will leap down and run, often killing any dog that stands in its way. A prudent hunter will, on such occasions, tie up his hounds before shooting a treed cougar.

The most important coon hounds are the black and tan, the bluetick, the English, the redbone, and the Plott. All are about the same size as the American foxhound, although the black and tan can be slightly larger, and the Plott slightly smaller.

The black and tan is black with tan markings on the legs and face, and often has a white blaze on the chest. Its ears are long and floppy, and it weighs 60 to 75 lb (27 to 34 kg). It is relatively slow, shows great determination, and can withstand the cold well. Black and tans take the scent from the ground and, with their fine deep, resonant booming voices, show evidence of their bloodhound ancestry. They are the oldest of the coon-hound breeds.

The bluetick has a bluish tinge over the whole body but is generally whitish and is tipped with tan points. It is less trim and racy-looking than the Walker but makes an excellent big-game hound, learning characteristically to run a trail well at a very early age.

The English hound is sometimes—helpfully—known as the redtick, being reddish where the bluetick is blue. Not such a showy hunter as some of the other coon hounds, this one is unswervingly steady and has a good record of finding a trail and treeing its quarry.

The redbone is similar in size to the bluetick and redtick, and to the American foxhound, if a little heavier. A typical color is a rusty red all over, and white spots are permissible on the toes and chest; although records are not complete, the breed is thought to owe its color to Irish hounds, perhaps setters, in the last quarter of the nineteenth century. It trails well, is skillful with raccoons, and makes an excellent bear hound, too. A good bear pack will combine redbones and Plotts.

Plotts are attributed to one Jonathan Plott, an emigrant from Germany to the Smoky Mountains of North Carolina in the mid-seventeenth century. The hounds he brought with him proved to be exceptionally good at hunting the black bear, which abounded in their new homeland, and their fame spread throughout the late eighteenth and nineteenth centuries, and then dwindled, perhaps because the Plott family was not interested in commercial exploitation of the breed, preferring to breed the hounds for themselves and their acquaintances. In the twentieth century, after the wild boar had been introduced into the Smoky Mountains, Plott hounds again became famous. Like their German ancestors, they are exceptionally fine boar hounds and are now used to hunt both boar and bear, as well as other game. Good Plott hounds are found throughout North America, and many have been bought by hunters in Europe.

The breed's shoulder height varies from about 21 to 25 inches (53 to 61 cm) and its weight from 45 to 60 lb (20 to 27 kg). The dog is stocky, very muscular, and has very strong jaws. It is brindled, that is, streaked with black and brown, over most of the body. There is usually a dark or black saddle, and there may be white points on the feet, chest, or both. A lighter shade appears in the occasional litter. This paler hue is said to be the result of the only out-cross that ever occurred—the breeding of a Plott many years ago with an outstanding bear hound from Georgia.

(Left) **COON HOUND.**
(Below) **ENGLISH FOXHOUND.**
(Opposite) **BEAR HOUND.**

Chapter 2
Training Hunting Dogs

Sten Christoffersson

As indicated in the previous chapter, most of the world's hunting dogs can be divided into five categories: scent hounds and sight hounds, pointing bird dogs, flushers (various breeds of spaniel), and retrievers. The last three have partly similar assignments: for example, a spaniel should be able to retrieve, while a retriever is sometimes asked to flush game, and most hunters want a pointer to be good at retrieving the birds that are shot over it.

Besides those groups, use is made in many countries of "earth dogs", primarily terriers but also the dachshund, to work underground when hunting chiefly foxes and badgers. In Scandinavia and northern Asia, for hunting elk, capercaillie and grouse, spitz dogs are employed to engage the quarry and keep it in sight until the hunter arrives, guided by the dog's barking. Sight dogs, too, are still used on the grassy plains of South America, in Canada, in Russia, on the Asian steppes and in Great Britain. A few breeds, such as Bavarian and Hanoverian tracking dogs, are specialized to follow the scent of injured hoofed game.

The types of hunting dog differ in their methods of hunting due to genetic factors. A pointer, for instance, has a natural instinct to stand tensely when it scents a bird, whereas a hound inherits the capacity to pursue game stubbornly as it gives tongue. But in addition, all hunting dogs require careful training before they can be considered ready for the field. Training allows the hunter to control the dog's innate urges so that it increases his or her chances of coming within shooting distance of the quarry.

Basic training is intended to make a young dog obedient and teach it habits that facilitate daily cooperation with a human being. If begun in time, the training has further effects which are even more important than specific activities. Once the dog learns clearly whose will is to be obeyed, it continues in future to regard the trainer as its pack leader, to pay attention and to please him. These fundamental lessons are generally the same for every breed of hunting dog.

The next stage is specialized training of a dog for the tasks that are to confront it during the hunt. This training is not equally identical for all types of dog. Although flushers and pointers certainly demand the most instruction, many hounds succeed largely in "training" themselves.

However, a first-class hunting dog is not only the product of fine genes and fastidious education. Substantial experience of hunting is necessary as well. Few dogs get this far until they are at least three years old, and the majority reach their peak of development at the age of four to seven – after which their performance diminishes with their strength. Frequently, a dog compensates for declining physique by relying on its great experience and can perform excellently in the field even at ten or twelve. To be sure, not many dogs can manage more than a short hunt when they have become teenagers.

Essential rules

The best conditions for training a hunting dog are established by keeping these principles in mind:

1. It is crucial to choose the pup from a line with proven aptitude for hunting. There is no way to make a clever hunter out of a dog that does not have the right predisposition.

The choice is seldom hard when dealing with breeds which are used only for hunting, like German pointers and Swedish foxhounds. Yet numerous breeds of hunting dog have also become popular as pets. If breeding is focused on other goals than the dog's ability to hunt, many of the key qualities for hunting disappear, and surprisingly soon. Examples of breeds which have thus been partly ruined for hunting are the dachshund, most terriers, all spaniels and retrievers, and various other bird dogs. Such pets are so lacking in hunting instincts that they no longer have any potential for development into acceptable helpmates for a hunter with high demands. Nonetheless, in most of these breeds, strains of good hunting dogs still exist, and it is from these that a hunter should select his dog.

2. Dogs learn mainly through repetition. They do not possess our powers of insight, and cannot understand why they ought to behave in a particular way. Nor do they learn anything by seeing an already trained dog perform the acts in question. Even if the dog is superb material, the training must be well-designed and systematically organized in order to yield results. Ideally, the training should go forward at a moderate pace without major setbacks. No practice can be too easy in the beginning. The degree of difficulty must be increased so slowly that the dog never has a problem in grasping what is required of it.

When such training is based on solid leadership, the need for punishment scarcely arises. If the trainer occasionally has to show dissatisfaction, it is usually enough to give a verbal reprimand or a sharp pull on the neck skin. Whoever feels that tougher methods are called for in dog training has chosen the wrong breeder and obtained an insufficiently cooperative pup, or else is himself an impatient and unscientific trainer.

3. Teach the dog correct behavior from the outset. For instance, if it has grown up with the freedom to jump on furniture or run in and out through doors, it will have far more trouble unlearning those things than if it had initially learned certain restrictions. A sound rule is never to let the pup do what it should not do as an adult dog. Then it will acquire good habits that last a lifetime. Just as in raising children, if the young have first been taught regular times, proper conduct and politeness, this behavior will become automatic.

For the same reason, a young bird dog should never be allowed to hunt game even as a pup. Neither should it be exposed to game until its obedience is so well ingrained that the handler can control his dog.

Not all hunters agree with this view, and some still think that one must let a bird dog hunt game at first in order to fire its lust for hunting. But a hunting dog should have the lust in its blood, and therefore does not need such firing – which unbalances the dog in game situations and creates serious problems in its subsequent training. The trainer then has to break the dog of a bad habit before he can teach it correct habits. Moreover, the wrong behavior will linger beneath the surface in the dog and, sooner or later, will erupt and cause misbehavior while hunting.

Bringing up pups and training leadership

A little pup is, in fact, highly responsive to teaching already when it is brought home from the breeder. Understanding how to exploit this early learning ability will yield much greater success, in training a hunting dog, than not trying to influence the dog actively until it is over half a year old.

It is extremely important, though, to realize that the pup at a tender age should not be submitted to training in the word's ordinary sense. Instead, one must do small exercises together with the pup, which it finds enjoyable and feasible. The exercises should be interrupted for a week or two if the pup shows the slightest sign of withdrawal, boredom or fear. If it fails, it should of course never be punished. Therefore, organize the practice so that the pup cannot fail, and always give it lavish praise when it does an exercise more or less correctly. Thus it will be eager to please and to work with joy and spontaneity.

Summoning, sitting, and simple fetching are quite appropriate for early training of a pup. Likewise, it can soon be taught to avoid jumping on furniture, entering particular rooms, and so on. Even if it is to stay in kennels as an adult, these exercises should be done carefully and consistently. The first three or four months of its life are the period when bonding is established between the dog and man. Hence, a pup should never stay alone in a kennel more than briefly and sporadically. If it is not often in contact with people who both display friendliness and place definite demands, it will never feel the right affinity with humans and submit to them. Then the very basis for future obedience and cooperativeness is absent.

One does not become a pack leader by constantly being friendly, obliging, and passing out candy. This approach makes a pup regard one as weak and ingratiating. It will grow independent and, in time, might even try to take over the leadership. Be lavish with your praise, patting and sweets, yet only when the pup has achieved something you asked of it. The most effective way to be seen as an unquestioned pack leader is to be firm but fair, and to remain the one who sets limits for what the pup may and may not do. You thus earn the dog's respect quickly, and gain its attentiveness much more readily than if you attempt to bribe it.

A useful exercise is to accustom the pup to a summoning signal, for instance by blowing on a whistle at each meal. The pup then learns that summoning often results in something positive, and obeys the signal gladly in other situations too. Together with this exercise, the pup can also easily be accustomed to sitting at the food bowl and waiting.

Naturally, such exercises do not by themselves render the dog any better at hunting; still, they have enormous value. The aim is to get the pup used, at an early age, to its will being permanently subordinated to that of man. Soon it understands exactly what is expected of it, comes happily at a signal when meals are served, and sits spontaneously when the food bowl is placed in front of it. This is the time to let the pup wait for the precious word that permits it to eat the delicacies. After a while, it looks up wonderingly at the handler, who only then gives the word. Before long, the pup learns that it must look alertly at its handler in order to begin eating, and the foundation is laid for attentiveness elsewhere as well.

Car training

All hunting dogs must be able to ride in a vehicle without feeling sick. One should thus not neglect to accustom the pup early on short car trips. Most people prefer to transport their dogs in the rear of a station-wagon or all-terrain vehicle, but this is the least suitable place if the pup has any tendency to get sick. Curves and swerves are felt much more keenly at points farther from the car's centre of gravity. It is better to place the pup on the floor next to the driver, near the centre of gravity as well as to human contact.

On the first trips, of course, two people should be in the car, so that the driver can concentrate on the road. The pup soon grows used to staying on the floor if it is prevented from jumping onto the seat. Gradually it learns to remain there even when the car is left parked briefly. Keep in mind that the weather need be only moderately warm for the car's interior to become dangerously hot if left with closed windows. Once the dog is properly accustomed to riding and leaps willingly into the car, it can ride in a cage at the rear.

A good way to strengthen leadership is always to make the dog sit at the threshold and wait for permission before running out. *English springer spaniel.*

(Left) Teach a hunting dog from the outset that it must stay in the car until it is told to jump out. *Brittany.*

(Right) Obedience training promotes attentiveness and cooperativeness in the dog, and supports the handler's leadership role. *Drever – a Scandinavian breed of hound, used mainly for roe-deer.*

Gun training

Accustoming a hunting dog to shooting before it first goes on a hunt is very important. This is all the more true of bird dogs which, unlike hounds for example, are in the midst of the activity during a hunt and experience shooting only a few metres from them. A gun-shy dog is obviously useless for hunting. While gun-shyness is rare among dogs from established hunting lines, it happens that a hunting dog can become gun nervous, showing aversion to the work and sneaking away if a shot is heard nearby. These tendencies are almost as bad as actual gun-shyness, but can be prevented by gradually getting the pup used to shooting.

Begin training with a starting pistol. Many pups show no reaction if a pistol is shot close to them, but for safety's sake the initial shots should be at a distance of fifty metres or more. A second person should be present to play with the pup when the shot is fired, and the pup must continue to play without showing any notice of the shot. If the pup does not react negatively, another shot can be fired at the same distance. By repeating the exercise daily, and gradually decreasing the distance, one soon finds the pup so accustomed that it pays no attention if the pistol is fired nearby while, for instance, it eats. One can then change cautiously to a shotgun and repeat the whole procedure, although very close shots should be delayed until the dog's training for hunting is well under way.

Obedience training

A dog's lust for hunting was formerly often believed to be inhibited by obedience training. This is certainly not the case. An obedient hunting dog is a more effective assistant, as it can be brought to hunt together with the hunter instead of independently wherever it likes. Obedience training also strengthens leadership, bonding the hunter and dog in a manner that makes them an efficient team.

"Sit!" Simple obedience training, such as sitting and summoning, should be practiced carefully during the pup's first weeks in its new home, as already noted. The great majority of pups will automatically sit if a food bowl, a tasty morsel, or something else interesting is held above and in front of them. If the pup tries to jump up, the hand is retracted quickly. When the pup sits down, it is calmly served what it wants. This exercise is repeated, but with the command to "sit". As a rule, the pup will sit immediately at the command.

It can be appropriate to raise one's hand at the same time as the command is spoken. This is especially useful for bird dogs, which must be made to sit or lie down with the sole command of an arm lifted at some distance. The bird dog's stop signal, a short and very firm blow on a whistle, can be introduced as soon as the pup understands sitting at the word and the hand gesture.

The pup may also be taught to sit by laying a hand on its chest and then, with a friendly but solid push of the other hand, lowering its rump while giving the "sit" command. Regardless of which method is used, a main point is not to let the pup stand up before it receives permission. During initial practice with the command, little harm is done if it gets up spontaneously. Yet once it knows what is required, the pup must gradually be taught to stay put as long as the trainer wishes.

Train the pup, too, in sitting at a distance. Begin at a few metres, and do not become angry if, in the first attempts, it runs forward and sits beside the handler. Eventually it will realize what is expected of it.

"Here!" Every hunting dog should be able to heed a summons during a hunt, when it is within hearing distance of its handler. For bird dogs, this is an absolute demand. The training can suitably begin early by attracting the pup with its name, or by blowing the call (often a rapid series of short notes) on a whistle. If it gets a morsel each time it comes directly, the pup acquires a positive attitude to the summons from the outset, and obeys unhesitatingly. By calling it from a crouching posture, one can increase its desire to come instantly. A wise measure, already now, is to hold one's arms spread horizontally at the sides when calling the pup. This is the accepted gesture for a summons, and after some repetition the pup will gladly come as soon as it sees one's open arms.

Almost every time the pup comes, it should immediately be released, so that it does not identify summoning with leashing. One must also avoid calling the pup in situations where one is not quite certain that it will obey. By thus establishing perfect obedience to the summons, one lays a good basis for continuing this training.

The use of candy should be gradually decreased, and the next step is to call the pup when it is busy with something else. Since the demands on the dog are being raised, one has to be completely sure that it hears the signal and knows what this means. Moreover, the dog must be at least half a year old. If it does not come immediately, it gets a stern "sit" command, and must stay put until it turns its attention to the handler. Only

(Above left) By squatting when you call the dog, its desire to come is increased. *English springer spaniel.*

(Above right) All hunting dogs must learn to walk calmly alongside. *English springer spaniel.*

All hunting dogs must learn to walk calmly alongside. *Drever.*

then is the summons repeated, perhaps from a shorter distance than the first time. Probably the dog will come without delay and, of course, it should be praised warmly.

"Heel!" Even if many of us do not think it matters much if a hunting dog pulls on the leash, most would undoubtedly agree that it is more comfortable to have a dog which can walk tidily to heel. But the issue is not only for comfort: there is an important safety aspect. With a loaded gun in one hand, and in the other a dog that pulls and strains, sometimes leaping in front of the hunter's feet, a serious danger arises for both him and the dog, as well as for anybody in the vicinity.

Granted, a hunting dog need not walk with its nose right beside the handler's left knee. Perfect docility is admirable, but is necessary only for pure obedience dogs. As long as a hunting dog always holds itself on a slack leash at the hunter's side, this is sufficient. If one intends to be very careful, the habit can also be taught early. A start may be made already when the pup is three or four months old. However, training to "heel" should be left until "sit" is firmly established.

The best approach is to sit the pup down, couple it to a light and supple leash, then walks a few steps while trying - with one's voice and body language – to make it keep a fairly smooth pace at one's left side. If this goes badly, a piece of candy in the hand can be helpful. But the pup should not get the candy before one has stopped again and it sits at the left.

Two things are important to remember here. First, do not begin by demanding that the pup walks perfectly at your side. Second, walk only a few steps to start with, then end the lesson by releasing the pup from the "sit" command and rewarding it with patting and perhaps candy.

A choke-chain is absolutely forbidden in these early exercises. This type of collar is a correction aid, and to be corrected the dog must be aware that it has done wrong. Otherwise it becomes afraid and loses trust in the handler, learning nothing at all. One has to steer the little pup gently so that it finds itself mostly in place during the promenade.

Equally essential is to praise the pup whenever it acts correctly. Otherwise it cannot comprehend or learn anything. By alternating between "Heel!" - while pulling the pup to the left side - and sweet praise when it gets into place, one shows the pup what is expected of it, and soon it adapts. Eventually it will also understand that, when one commands "Heel!" and begins to walk, it must follow tidily at the left side.

Do not forget that a little pup should never be subjected to regular training sessions. It is sufficient to walk the pup properly just once or twice a day, at first only a few metres and, when six months old, a hundred metres. Each time, the pup should then be released in an orderly manner and played with. Thus it will perk up whenever the leash-training begins, since it knows that fun will follow.

Once the young dog is mature enough for regular sessions, it already knows what is required, so the training will be both faster and more effective. If the dog tends to disobey, you can now use a choke-chain directly, although with moderation. If the dog pulls on the leash, it should immediately be called to heel and, a split second later, corrected with a strong jerk on the leash, so that it gets in place at the left side. To jerk first and call next is a big mistake, since the dog will not learn that it can avoid the pull by instantly obeying the command.

Training for the hunt

After the obedience training, one can start to prepare the dog purely for hunting. This is done to a varying extent, depending on the breed and the kind of use, as well as on the individual hunter's requirements for a dog. Given the further contrasts in how breeds of hunting dog are employed around the world, the training also differs between countries and continents.

Hounds
North American and European hounds work in distinct ways - and even within Europe, their kinds of use and methods of hunting are very diverse. In classic hunting in Great Britain, hounds hunt in large packs, followed by an often great number of unarmed hunting people. The latter may pursue the hunt on horseback, as when hunting foxes with foxhounds - or else on foot, as when going after hares with beagles, or mink with otterhounds. The same is done in France and some other Continental countries, but chiefly for hoofed game.

Scandinavia has a totally different, quite advanced culture of hunting with hounds. Frequently a single hunter is involved, and seldom do more than two or three participate. Only one hound is used, and has to work alone in finding the game, then drive it patiently at a modest tempo while giving tongue constantly. The hunter takes his stand where he thinks the quarry will come past. Fast, high-legged dogs of the foxhound type are trained to ignore hoofed game, and are used solely for hare and fox. Hoofed game, primarily roe deer, are hunted with low breeds such as the dachshund, drever and basset, whose slow pace ensures that the quarry is not unduly alarmed.

Hounds of a type that has gained general use on the Continent and in Scandinavia are short-driving breeds, such as German terriers and spaniels. These hunt mainly deer and wild boar. They bark while chasing, but by no means as long as the "real" hounds do. Since they are mostly used in variable terrain and small wooded areas, a few minutes' chase is usually enough for one of the accompanying hunters to get a shot.

North America has a special type of hound to pursue species like the raccoon and puma, which tend to flee up a tree. The dog then marks the place by barking to lead the hunter there. Jackrabbits and similar species, as well as hoofed game in some states, are hunted with beagles and other kinds of hound. In many parts of the United States, though, it is forbidden to hunt hoofed game with hounds.

As a rule, little preliminary training is needed to make a hound hunt properly. Hounds are independent breeds that gladly take off by themselves when released in a forest, and begin to hunt when they find game. The first hunts are normally short and hesitant, but the dog becomes ever more efficient as it acquires experience.

Hares are notably hard to pursue, even for an experienced hound. All hare species share the habit of sometimes taking a long side-hop, often after doubling back to follow their own trail for several metres.

The beagle is a hound breed with great interest in hares.

A radio direction finder can help to locate lost dogs, but it should not be used to hunt more effectively.

The German hunting terrier is a versatile breed that not only serves as an earth dog and pursues deer or wild boar, but also retrieves.

Moreover, hares leave a much weaker scent than do foxes and hoofed game. Thus, to develop a truly clever and good-tracking hound, one should develop its hunting on hares. Lacking its experience, a hound that is trained on hoofed game frequently becomes confused when the scenting conditions are poor and the trail is difficult to follow.

If the dog will not be allowed to hunt hoofed game, training it on hares is naturally all the more important. Such a dog must be carefully controlled so that it is not tempted to chase forbidden game. By always praising its interest in hares, but scolding it for any notice of a roe deer's scent, the lesson is soon taught. High-legged Scandinavian scent-hounds have been bred for generations to concentrate on hares and foxes, until today many of them are oblivious to hoofed game.

In countries where two or more hounds are left to hunt together, the young dog can be released with an experienced dog, so as to learn from its companion. However, this method is not recommended for a dog that will have to work alone. It must learn to seek independently on the ground for the faintest scent of game, and to follow the scent until it makes contact with the animal. Neither should the handler help it too much. Best take the dog to a place in the forest where game should be nearby, sit down on a tree stump with a good book, and let the dog do the rest. Even when the dog loses the scent, you should only encourage the dog, not try actively to help. During a real hunt, the hound must solve all such problems on its own. Whoever helps his dog during the hunting-in stage will pay dearly during hunting seasons.

In recent years it has become increasingly common to locate hounds with the aid of telemetry. A tiny transmitter is fixed to the dog's collar. A receiver enables the hunter to take a bearing and determine both the direction and distance to the dog. This, of course, is a great tool for rescuing a lost dog, but is clearly unethical if used to locate the dog while hunting and thereby improve one's chances of downing the quarry. Nor should a direction-finder be used to recover the dog at the hunting day's end. Otherwise the dog will accustom itself to being taken out of the forest, instead of learning to look for its handler when it can no longer hunt the game.

Earth dogs

In Europe, earth dogs are universally employed to hunt fox and badger. These two wild game species call for rather different tecnique of the dog, and hence it is rare for a dog to be equally good for both.

A fox dog should be hot-tempered, often climbing out of one hole and entering another. Hard pressure is thus put on the fox, forcing it to leave the den, frequently just as the dog is shifting position. Then the hunter gets a chance to shoot the fox.

A badger dog has a quite distinct tactic. It lies in front of the burrow and keeps the badger there, by constantly barking and sporadically attacking. The hunter digs down and executes the badger at close range with a small-calibre pistol.

In the United States, earth work is far less widespread, although earth dogs are often used to hunt marmots.

Terriers were originally bred to work in underground holes, and their name derives from Latin for the earth (*terra*). Today the majority tend to be pets, but strains with excellent earth-dog qualities still exist among Jack Russell terriers, border terriers, fox terriers and German hunting terriers. Even dachshunds began as earth dogs, having been named in German for the badger (*Dachs*).

The training of earth dogs is aimed chiefly at making the dog so obedient that it can be called out of the hole. Hunting with a disobedient earth dog is very frustrating. A fox hunt, for example, becomes meaningless if the dog meets a badger in the earth and stubbornly stays there. Unlike foxes, a badger is usually impossible for the dog to bolt, so the day can easily be ruined.

Training is best done in special "earths" above ground, with branched board tunnels, through which the dog can find its way to a confined "chamber" where a tame badger or fox has been placed. The dog soon learns to reach the chamber even when the passage is impeded by narrow places, sand banks or water traps. At several points the handler can open lids in the tunnels to encourage the dog, or to take action if it has not obeyed a command.

Under no circumstances should an earth dog be too keen. Dogs that go into battle with badgers are unsuitable as earth dogs. Courage, stubbornness and intelligence are the hole dog's weapons, not thirst for blood and defiance of death.

Elkhounds and barking bird dogs

In Scandinavia and northern Russia, moose and bear, as well as martens and forest birds, are hunted with diverse types of spitz dogs. These are normally supposed to find the game and lead the hunter to it by barking continuosly. In Russia, various forms of laika are commonly used as all-round hunting dogs. In Scandinavia, several big breeds of dog hunt for moose and bear, while the smaller breeds hunt for capercaillie and black grouse, martens and – formerly – squirrels.

Training of a hunting spitz begins by accustoming the pup to the forest. It is taken there as often as possible and allowed to follow its own initiatives, as long as it stays in contact with the handler. A future elk-hound must slowly grow acquainted with the scent of moose, but should not be released on their trail before it approaches one year of age. Moose are huge animals, and have been known to become irritated by dogs and attack them. Unless the dog is well developed physically, it may be injured or frightened off.

Once the dog finds its first moose and begins to take a stand by barking, the hunter should hurry to the spot, although cautiously to avoid scaring the moose. If the moose is not motionless in front of the barking dog, the handler must wait. When the dog manages to make the moose stop, you have to get in position quickly and shoot. The dog must learn, from the outset, that there will be no rewards if it fails to hold the moose in place.

If the dog stops a moose that is not to be shot, you must carefully lure the dog away from its stand, so that the moose does not panic and run off with the dog in pursuit. Conscientious training of obedience in the pup and young dog is an important requirement for success when calling the elk-hound from a stand. The dog is generally aware of whether the handler is nearby, and sometimes leaves the moose to regain contact with him. This moment should be exploited by quietly leashing the dog and sneaking away.

After the dog has become experienced, one can delay the shot longer and, for further training, even let the dog keep the elk in place for several hours. An elkhound is not flagrantly aggressive toward the moose – which does not normally pay much attention to the dog either, but continues its calm browsing, apparently bored by the dog's incessant barking.

A barking bird dog is taught to hunt in rather the same manner. However, the training can begin outdoors at home, by enticing the pup to bark at a bird's wing that is hung up on a tree and, finally, is lowered to the pup when it has barked constantly for a while.

During its training sessions in the forest, when the dog encounters birds that are feeding and forces them to fly, it pursues them until it loses sight of them. Early in the season, the birds do not fly very far, but usually settle in a tree close to the place where they were flushed. As soon as the dog has located a bird, it stands and barks beneath the tree.

The hunter must then make an extremely cautious approach, to get in shooting position without scaring the bird. Young dogs tend to have great problems in accurately locating the bird, and often bark under the wrong trees or return to bark at the flushing place. Nor do they usually bark for long. Thus one should waste no time in reaching the spot and trying to locate the bird, which is frequently quite difficult to see if it sits in a pine or fir tree, seldom huddling close to the trunk. If the dog goes on barking when the hunter finds the bird, he should shoot the bird as a reward for the dog. Success, the dog must realize, is attained only by barking continuously under the right tree.

With time, the dog also learns to locate birds that have flown a long way. An experienced dog can often use its hearing to find the tree where a bird has alighted, and display a phenomenal ability to tell exactly where

This type of bird dog helps the hunter by finding birds and barking beside the tree they occupy. *Finnish spitz, with capercaille cock.*

the bird is sitting in the tree. But this takes quite a while, and the handler should never let his own hunting lust predominate, but shoot only when the dog has done good work.

Pointing bird dogs

Hunting with pointers started in Europe, where this sport has been popular for centuries. At first, the dogs were used to hunt with falcons or at night. When weapons to shoot birds in flight emerged during the 1700s, shooting over pointers evolved rapidly into the accepted form of hunting that is still practiced across much of the world. The dogs work almost exclusively for hunting gallinaceous birds, but woodcock and snipe are also shot with pointers, and some hunters even use theirs for small furred game such as hare and rabbit.

It cannot be doubted that bird dogs, both pointers and flushers, demand the most training among all hunting dogs. For hunting over a bird dog comprises many steps, which require thorough training before the dog can master them fully. Luckily, the bird-dog breeds benefit more than other dogs from training, and this makes the process easier.

When the bird flushes, the pointing dog must stop or lie down. *German wirehaired pointer.*

A pointer has to scour the terrain effectively, and methodically. When it finds a sqatting bird, it must go on point – that is, stop where it scents the bird and stay until the hunter orders it to move. When the hunter arrives, he commands the dog to rode in and put up the bird. As soon as the bird takes off, the dog must freeze again. If the bird is shot, the hunter can command the dog to retrieve and deliver the prey to hand.

Furthermore, a pointer is asked to "back" – immediately go on point when it sees another dog pointing a bird. When hunting in thick cover, there is also an advantage of having a dog that reports – leaving the point and going to the hunter, then leading him to the bird's haunt. This last trait, though rather unusual, is highly valued, especially by forest-bird hunters.

Hunters in different parts of the world, however, do not require exactly the same things of their pointers. Danish and Scandinavian hunters want the dog to rode out the bird briskly and boldly on command, whereas Continental and British hunters are content if it is done at a slow pace while they are right next to the dog. In North America, no conditions of flushing exist whatever: instead, the dog is commanded to stay put as the hunter himself goes forward to flush the bird. Nor is retrieving a universal rule, as regards the British setter breeds and the pointer; in these breeds' homeland, retrieving by the dog is not called for at all.

Pointing as well as backing, and sometimes retrieving, must be inborn traits in a pointer, just like the interest in birds and the will to search the ground for them. On the other hand, any dog must be taught to stand "staunch" patiently after it has found a bird, not to chase birds or other game, or to run in on a bird that is shot in front of it. Moreover, the training to retrieve is fairly extensive.

To succeed in developing a reliable and cooperative pointing dog, one should prepare it as a pup, by training situations of hunting. This must not be done on real game in the field, but under artificial circumstances at home. Probably the most common error when training pointers is to bring the dog, before it is completely obedient, out into areas with wild game. Such a dog will inevitably chase hares, rabbits or flushed birds, and run in when birds take wing or are shot. A young dog naturally enjoys the scenario, and its trainer is thus faced with almost insurmountable difficulties when he or she later tries to make the dog respect, in other words not to chase after, game.

By being careful in the first half-year to teach the pup many good habits, and to prevent its acquiring bad habits that contradict the behavior one wants it to have when hunting, one prepares for the actual practical training as competently as possible. Good habits learned early have been proved to last often throughout life, just as bad habits readily become permanent and are therefore always hard to eradicate.

The practical training itself is foreshadowed when the pup is a few months old, with the aid of a fishing rod and a dried wing. This is normally from some wild gallinaceous bird, but a tame chicken wing serves as well. The pup can easily be induced to point at the sight of the wing. If it does not hold the point, the wing is jerked up in the air and disappears from the pup's sight. It then learns quickly that nothing is gained by trying to catch the wing instead of pointing. As soon as the pup points at the wing, it must be praised in a calm and friendly voice, so that it understands it is doing right but does not get excited.

Once the point is established, the pup is made to advance and "flush" the wing – which again disappears into the blue, while the handler carefully sits or lies the pup down. The wing may also slowly "scuttle away", whereupon the pup must follow and, once more, stop when the wing does. If it tries to rush when the wing moves, this vanishes into the air as before. Thus, at an early stage, the pup can be taught the basic behavior for dealing with birds, which facilitates its real lessons on the training grounds.

The intention is not to create a finished hunting dog at home on the lawn with a bird's wing, but to implant the foundations of hunting behaviour. When the practical training seriously begins in the field, the dog rapidly learns to point also at the scent of birds, and to respect birds taking off. However, one must start training under conditions as controlled as possible, and initially a few metres of line on the dog's collar are desirable. The first times that the dog points birds, the handler can carefully approach and grab the line. If the situation is under control, the dog receives quiet and friendly praise, before it is commanded forward to flush the birds. Should the dog grow eager and want to chase after the ascending birds, it can easily be restrained with the line.

One has to avoid, though, pulling hard on the line or causing other discomfort for the dog. Otherwise it connects the discomfort with the birds, and may become increasingly unwilling to flush them. This sort can never turn into a truly good hunting dog. Instead, the line ought to be used for whoaing the dog as softly as possible, while one simultaneously gives the stop signal - and when the dog has stopped, it should instantly be praised. Thereby it learns much faster to understand what one wants. A fully trained dog must freeze at the rise of birds as soon as the stop signal is given. Dogs with comprehensive training do not even need any signal from their handlers. The flutter of wings or the glimpse of a bird in the air is enough for them to stop.

People lacking access to bird-rich grounds for dog training can, as a very good alternative, train with quail or partridge that are liberated. Tame pigeons are also usable to train bird dogs. These may be placed in special cages which are opened by employing a small radio transmitter.

At the beginning, it is crucial to establish the dog's behavior properly before embarking on a real shooting expedition. The handler must not shoot birds over the dog until it has flushed numerous birds without pursuing them. Whoever breaks this self-evident rule is bound to suffer setbacks, and seldom acquires a dog that works well in hunting. The reason is simple. If the dog learns clearly what is demanded of it by doing the right things repeatedly, it understands the handler's dissatisfaction when it does wrong. If it is allowed to do wrong initially, it has no idea how to behave correctly – which, of course, means that getting angry at it will not help.

Neither should the dog be permitted to retrieve when birds are first shot over it. Otherwise it soon associates the shot with retrieving, and runs in after the bird at the sound of the gun.

In order to maintain a high level of training during the dog's whole active life, one should devote a few days before each shooting season to training the different steps. And while shooting, one must keep watch for defects emerging in the dog's behaviour, so that they can be corrected in time. How a bird dog is taught to retrieve will be described later in the text.

Flushing dogs

A flusher's task is to raise game directly, without first pointing. It must not run after the flushed quarry, either. To give the hunter a chance of shooting the flushed game, the dog must never search farther from the hunter than 25 or at most 30 metres. The flusher is nearly always a spaniel, usually an English springer spaniel or a cocker spaniel. However, in the United States, retrievers are also often used as flushers.

Hunting with flushers has its roots in the British Isles, where the diverse breeds of spaniel originated. This form of hunting is undoubtedly most popular in Great Britain, holding a strong lead over hunting with pointers. The explanation, in great measure, is certainly that the spaniel is the most effective dog for confined, well-stocked grounds, where game frequents dense hedges or thorny blackberry thickets, high grass or tall stands of fern. Besides, the spaniel is unbeatable at hunting rabbits, as its meticulous hunting method lends itself to this specialised game finding.

A spaniel has flushed a rabbit and stops just when it flees.

The flushing dog must quickly get the bird into the air...

...but as soon as the bird is on the wing, the dog must stop or sit down.
English springer spaniel.

In the rest of Europe as well, birds and minor furred game are hunted with flushers, while in North America spaniels are used mainly to hunt birds. On both continents, pheasants are the wild birds most often shot by spaniel-hunters. But partridge, various American quail species, blackcock, capercaillie, grouse, and even woodcock are regularly shot with the help of spaniels.

Training of a flusher is, in principle, as extensive as that of a pointer. First and foremost, the spaniel must be taught to keep itself searching near its handler. Steadiness in the presence of game is, to be sure, another essential lesson before the dog is taken hunting. In addition, the dog must learn to retrieve furred game and birds alike.

The training should begin very early, by imparting good habits to the pup and, at all costs, ensuring that it does not learn things which will be absolutely forbidden during a hunt. Thus, the pup must not be allowed to run about as it pleases, or to stray far from the handler when it chooses, any more than it should run after game or tame birds. Granted that it ought to play and romp, and have a happy upbringing, one must constantly shun the curse of condoning behavior that may hinder its future training for its shooting career.

When the young dog has accustomed itself to the noise of a starting pistol, it should learn to sit down when a shot is fired. While the dog is busy with something else, let off a shot with your arm outstretched. The dog is to regard the arm as a "sit" signal, when the sound makes it look around in surprise. Possibly a vocal command or a whistle will be needed at first. Soon the dog regards the shot as a "sit" signal, and obeys at the crack of the gun. Usually a spaniel sits much faster at a shot than at other such commands. A dog that always sits when a shot is fired is less likely to run in, compared with dogs which have only learned to connect the shot with a dead bird falling nearby.

After this preparation it is time to train questing. A spaniel with good

hunting blood in its veins has a natural inclination to search the surroundings, and likes to scamper about in thick vegetation. This should definitely be encouraged, as long as the dog never strays too far away. When training, the handler should move very slowly through the terrain and see that the dog searches both open land and dense cover, without getting farther from him than 20 metres or so. The dog must conform to the handler, not vice versa. By occasionally changing direction, and even hiding if one thinks the dog has been inattentive, one teaches it to keep an eye on the handler and adapt itself to his movements. If the dog ever tends to stray too far, it is immediately stopped with a whistle and called in, then allowed to resume the search. A special "return" signal is worth teaching, especially for the training on open ground. There the spaniel must search with a regular zigzag pattern in front of its handler.

Initially the training is done only in gameless terrain, but eventually one can move on to game areas. Best start training on birds, either wild or released pheasant or partridge. Pigeons in cages that can be opened with a radio transmitter are also useful (as above for pointers). However, it is important that the dog's obedience be well established, so that if and when the young spaniel does meet game, the handler is able to stop the dog on the whistle.

When the dog first flushes a bird, it is usually too surprised to pursue. The next time, it will have caught on, and the handler must be ready to step in without a moment's thought. Inattention is a cardinal mistake when training a spaniel. One's eyes should be constantly on the dog. Then one soon manages to interpret its behaviour, and can tell when it finds a scent just before the bird flushes. By quickly getting close to the dog, one is able to intervene if necessary. A young dog that is properly trained will sit immediately at a signal when the bird rises. Otherwise it must be carried back to the flushing place, and sit there awhile before being sent on a new search. This calls for still greater readiness when the dog again finds game.

Gradually the dog learns what is expected of it. Given a talented animal and adequate opportunities for some weeks of training, one seldom has trouble in producing a dog that sits spontaneously without any signal when game is flushed.

Yet even the most scrupulous training can easily be ruined by starting to hunt too early with the dog. Not before it has shown itself on several occasions to be perfectly steady in game situations should the first bird be shot over it. In addition, no matter how calm it is, the dog must not initially be allowed to retrieve. If it runs in after the downed bird, firm and instant correction is the only alternative to rapid habituation – and one has to stop shooting over the dog until the training is markedly improved.

Retrieving

The question of how best to teach a hunting dog to retrieve is often discussed vehemently among hunters. Some claim that it can learn retrieving by playing. Others say the results are achieved by building the whole training on the dog's spontaneous urge to fetch things. Still others stick to the view that retrieving must be taught by the force method.

Successful training is always based upon the dog's aptitudes. Otherwise there would be no need to have different breeds of gundogs: one could train any dog for any task at all. Learning to retrieve is obviously no exception and, if it is to proceed at a resonable pace with acceptable results, the dog must have an inborn urge to retrieve. Why extreme compulsion in training should ever be required is therefore hard to understand. Nonetheless, relying entirely on the dog's own will to run and fetch a thrown object can be risky. In the field, one is not satisfied with a dog that only fetches when it wishes. A really good retriever must invariably do its utmost to find game that is shot.

To end up with a retriever that is dependable, as well as enthusiastic and eager to work, the training must be built on the dog's natural ability.

Base the retrieving training upon the dog's spontaneous urge to carry things in its mouth. *English springer spaniel.*

At the same time, though, one must be able to demand absolute obedience to the "retrieve" command. The art is to bring the dog through the training in such a manner that it neither forgets its duty, nor loses its joy and motivation to work.

Retrieving traits are most developed within the bird-dog breeds, but there are considerable distinctions between types of pointing, flushing, and retrieving bird dogs. Certain breeds and individuals have such a powerful urge to retrieve that the dog will tirelessly and gladly fetch the same object forever. Others have to be persuaded even that their mouths can be used to carry things.

In any case, not all retrievers are bird dogs. Virtually any breed of hunting dog can be taught with patience and encouragement to retrieve. Indeed, adept retrievers exist among dachshunds, hounds, spitz hunting dogs, and diverse terriers. Many members of the pet-dog breeds are also able to learn retrieving.

Early play at retrieving with a pup develops its natural talent and establishes a positive attitude toward the act. One should totally avoid placing demands, or else the early training yields more harm than benefit. The time will soon come to set up requirements and ask for complete obedience – but if this is done prematurely, the pup withdraws and shows reluctance to train.

Begin by rolling a tennis ball on the floor and letting the pup run after it. Most pups take the ball in their mouths and want to keep it awhile. If you choose a small room and position yourself right, you can gently catch the dog to praise it, and roll the ball again. Under no circumstances should you chase alongside the pup to take the ball. This would make the chase an amusement, so that the object retrieved is not given back. Instead the pup must be taught that the playing resumes when the ball is delivered to the handler. Then it soon learns to bring the ball voluntarily.

If the exercise fails, one should stop and try again a week later. An important point is to avoid growing angry at the pup, attempting to force it, or fighting with it. Some pups fetch the ball and return with it at an age of only eight to ten weeks, whereas others do so much later. One has to wait and see.

As a further principle, never let the pup run after the ball immediately: restrain it for a few seconds after the ball has stopped. Thus it learns, fairly rapidly, not to retrieve except at the command. Often already at three or four months of age, it acquires the habit of sitting nicely and watching for the "go" sign. If one teaches steadiness consistently, neither will the dog run off directly when it is adult. Early habits, both good and bad, easily become permanent behavior – a fact that can reward trainers who have foresight.

High standards for the delvery of should not be set at first. It matters little if the pup releases the ball before you take hold. Proper delivery can be taught to a young dog in due course. Trying to get everything perfect in the beginning is likely to destroy the pupil's pleasure of retrieving. Once you are quite sure that the pup always comes right back with the ball, the training may be moved to a larger room or outdoors. The exercises are then also made more difficult, in order to stimulate the dog and increase its eagerness. The ball is suitably replaced with a soft canvas dummy, of the kind sold in most dog-sport shops.

As the dog approaches a year of age, completion of the basic obedience training enables you to refine the delivery procedure. An unconditional rule of obedience must, however, be adopted. It is essential to separate this training, in both time and space, from the pleasure-emphasizing retrieval exercises with the dog previously. Otherwise, there is a serious risk of ruining the dog's desire to retrieve.

The training should now be moved back indoors. Sit beside the dog, hold the dummy in front of its nose, and command it to retrieve. Many

When the dog patiently awaits the command to retrieve...

...and does not hesitate to take the object when offered, it shows that it understands what is required of it. From then on, the handler can demand that the dog always obeys an order to retrieve.

dogs take the dummy already before the command is given. You should accept this only once or twice, and subsequently make sure that the dog awaits the command. While others take the dummy on command from the start, certain dogs appear not to understand what is meant, despite having retrieved hundreds of times when playing. Your response must be calm and friendly: put the dummy in the dog's mouth and praise it, then take back the dummy and praise it effusively. Even this dog will soon realize that it has to take at the command. But proceed cautiously with such a dog, so that it does not lose spirit.

Next, require the dog to keep the dummy for a few seconds, and gradually for an ever longer interval. At the command "let go" it should instantly release the dummy. Avoid hurrying, and organize the exercises over a number of days. Never make the training sessions longer than a few minutes.

If the dog spits out the dummy, it is stuffed decisively back into the dog's mouth with an instructive "hold". Especially at the beginning, praise is important when the dog places the dummy in your hand. However, you should always delay the praise until after the delivery, or the dog may drop the dummy in sheer ecstasy.

Now the dog is also taught the "hold" command, which can be used if it sometimes seems about to drop what it has retrieved. When the dog is good at sitting with the dummy in its mouth, you can go a few steps away from it, call it in, and make it sit before commanding "let go". Eventually, you can let it walk with the dummy in its mouth.

This method will not only yield a correct delivery, but teaches the dog what the word "fetch" means, and one can demand in future that the word be heeded. It is worth stressing that impatience, anger and violence should never be exhibited during the exercises. Face any hurdles with equanimity and solve the problems in an atmosphere of encouraging, though firm, friendliness.

Once the dog has learned consistently to obey the "fetch" command, to hold on as long as required, and to let go on command, it is time to connect the delivery with thrown objects. Then the dog will continue to retrieve rapidly and enthusiastically, yet deliver with discipline.

Scent training

For most hunters today, a tracking dog is an indispensable helper. Those who happen to wound an animal are rarely able to follow and kill it without assistance. Even if the shot is fatal, finding the prey can be difficult. A moose or deer, or a wild boar, may travel far after a perfect hit, becoming impossible to locate except by a clever dog. Pheasants that fall among dense bushes, or ducks that land in deep water, are also hard to recover unless a retriever is available. In several countries, the hunter is also now legally obliged to have a trained tracking dog in the field.

Often the same dog can be used to track both hoofed game and small game, but the delete technique itself is different. Tracking hoofed game calls for a dog that patiently seeks out the shot animal and leads the hunter to it. The hunter normally attaches a line to the dog. Commonly on the Continent, tracking dogs independently find the animal and then, in some manner, report the place to the hunter. They do so either by staying with the animal and barking to attract the hunter, or by coming back to the hunter and taking him there. Shooting dogs for small game always work independently. These are physically superior to the prey and, hence, must retrieve it to the handler.

An additional distinction between the techniques for Following the lines of hoofed and small game is that, when hunting the former, one

A tracking dog independently follows the injured animal. On finding it, the dog summons the hunter by barking continuously. Labrador retriever.

never sends the dog immediately after the shot. A large hoofed quarry might otherwise spend its last strength to run even farther, and perhaps be lost for good. By contrast, if one waits at least an hour after the shot, the wounded animal will have time to lie down, making it much easier to locate. A retriever is sent out straight after the shot, and can thus catch up faster with the wounded prey to collect it.

The most important part of training a tracking dog for hoofed game is scent training. A dog cannot be forced to follow a scent trail. All the tracking must flow from its own urge to follow a scent, either because it enjoys the process, or because it experiences a reward when the trail ends with a roe deer's hoof or the joy of a live retrieve.

A training scent is ordinarily laid by using a string to drag a deer's

hoof, while sprinkling or dropping blood along the trail. This is normally pig or cattle blood, which can be ordered in a food shop. The blood is divided into portions of a few decilitres and frozen.

One has to maintain an exact knowledge of where the trail leads. It must therefore be marked somehow, for instance with colorful strips of plastic, tied to clothes-pins that can be attached quickly as one passes. Carry them on a wire ring, hanging over your shoulder when the trail is laid.

For the dog, a line is needed, as well as a tracking harness or a broad tracking collar. Neither harness nor collar should be used in any other circumstances than tracking. The dog must associate them with this work. The line should be at least five metres long, and smooth on its surface to minimize friction against vegetation. Preferably it has a clear, bright color that is not obscured by dim light, in case one must occasionally let go of the line.

Begin by laying only short trails with plenty of blood. When a trail is completed, the dog is brought. Just before the tracking starts, the harness or collar is put on, and the holder points to the trail, commanding it to seek. At first the dog is baffled, but the scent of blood captures its interest. As soon as it takes some steps along the trail, it should be praised in a low voice. The praise is strengthened when the dog reaches the trail's end, which is marked by the hoof or a rolled-up deerskin. In little time, it will understand the meaning of the command. Gradually the trails are made longer, and ever less blood is used. The trails are also left for greater periods before bringing the dog. Not much more time will find the dog easily succeeding with a trail several hours old, hundreds of metres long.

A dog that has received diverse scent training, with trails of varying length and age, in different types of terrain and conditions of weather, possesses improved chances of managing a difficult recovery. But this is not to call it a fully-trained tracking dog. Artificial blood trails are not at all equivalent to the trail of a wounded beast. The only way to produce a truly smart tracking dog is to let it go on as many real trackings as possible, even when the hunter has seen the animal fall dead after a short flight.

To train a tracking dog at reporting is more complicated. Some dogs are naturally inclined to stop and bark when they come upon dead game. One can also entice the dog to bark whenever it arrives at a trail's end during the line training. If, in time, it barks voluntarily on arriving, it can be released a bit earlier on the next trail, to see whether it independently follows to the end and barks there. This will justify high hopes of getting the dog to report by barking in real situations of tracking as well.

However, the dog must be absolutely reliable and keep barking until the handler reaches it, regardless of the delay.

Training a dog to return and fetch the handler, after it has independently found the animal, is not as hard as one may believe. Before starting, the dog must be able both to track on a line and to retrieve. Briefly, training begins by teaching the dog to retrieve a decimetre-long strip of leather, or something similar, which has been placed on a rolled-up deerskin. At first, the exercises occur with the dog and handler right beside the skin. Then the dog is made to retrieve the strip from a few metres' distance. As it returns to the handler, he should not accept the strip, but go with the dog to the skin, where the delivery occurs.

Eventually, the skin is positioned out of sight, and a short trail is laid to the spot. The dog follows the scent and carries the strip to the handler. He encourages the dog to bring him to the skin, and accepts the strip with abundant praise. Later, the strip is fastened to the dog's collar by a short string, and the dog is sent toward the skin at a close distance, so that the handler has it in full view. When the dog reaches the skin and does not find any strip to retrieve, it discovers the strip at its collar, and takes this in its mouth. Once the dog is accustomed to these circumstances, the string is shortened, to prevent the strip from hanging down too far and getting in the way or snagging on vegetation.

This simple method yields, surprisingly soon, a dog that reports finding the animal by coming back to the handler with the strip in its mouth. It then shows the path to the animal, whereupon the strip is removed from its mouth. But the strip should never be attached to the tracking collar until the dog is to be sent tracking freely. Thus it will quickly learn to associate the strip with independently seeking a wounded quarry.

II Conservation

Chapter 1

Modern Trends in Game Management

Richard F. LaRocco

Conservation is an overused word today. Politicians, environmentalists, oil-company executives, housewives, and even schoolchildren talk of conservation—of the world's forests, its energy resources, its farmlands, its wildlife. To the average person, however, conservation means nothing more than making a resource last longer by reducing consumption of it. Yet it signifies much more, particularly to the sport hunter.

Conservation is more than simply preservation. It is wise *management*. And in the case of wildlife resources, it is the management of a supply of riches that will never end if cared for properly. An oil well, once partially drained, never fills again. A copper mine, once relieved of a single ounce of its metal, is reduced permanently. But a healthy, properly managed game population can supply man with meat and recreation, hide or feathers, for generations—forever. Wildlife is a renewable resource—a replenishable resource. As such, it is one of man's most valuable possessions and one of his most priceless treasures.

In Britain and Europe, with a conservation record many times longer than any in Africa, Asia, or the New World, landowners and gamekeepers have long been motivated by purely practical considerations, and recently, they have been joined by scientists in protecting this self-replacing wealth by further improving the art of wildlife management. Its practitioners have various objectives. Sometimes, their only purpose is to promote a particular species, to increase its numbers. This is often the case with rare or endangered animals, which are encouraged to multiply to lessen the threat of extinction. Sometimes, wildlife is managed to provide recreation, not only for those who shoot, but also for those who observe, such as bird-watchers and wildlife photographers. Most game birds and mammals are managed with human recreation in mind. Game animals, of course, also provide meat and often income for governments, landowners, tour operators, hunting guides, lodge and hotel owners, and others. Frequently, much of the revenue generated by the recreational use of wildlife is used to support and promote the wildlife. Sometimes, the only objective of wildlife management is to control: when red deer invade farms in parts of Europe or when waterfowl by the thousand sweep into the southern Canadian grainfields, their numbers must be controlled or crops will be destroyed.

Wildlife management is nothing new. Egyptian nobles hunted for sport, and it is likely that they reserved certain game species and choice hunting areas for their own use. In Europe, royal forest preserves have existed for a least twelve centuries. Genghis Khan restricted the kill of certain animals in short supply. American Indians used fire to promote the growth of deer browse long before the white man set foot in the New World in the fifteenth century.

Modern conservation had its start round another fire—a campfire deep in the wilds of North America's Yellowstone Valley in 1870. Round its flames were gathered a group of Montana citizens, who had organized an expedition into the region after having heard rumors of the Yellowstone Valley's natural wonders. The sight of these features was even more

A

B

inspiring and incredible than these men had thought possible. Though the explorers could have claimed the land under United States law and exploited it for their own profit, they decided that the Yellowstone region was too wondrous to be held in private hands. Talking round the campfire that September night, they decided to give the region to the people of the United States, giving birth to the idea of the world's first national park. Congress set aside Yellowstone National Park in 1872 as a "public park or pleasuring ground for the benefit and enjoyment of the people."

Soon, other parks were created: Yosemite and Sequoia in California, 1890; Mount Rainier in Washington, 1899; Crater Lake in Oregon, 1902; Wind Cave in South Dakota, 1903; Mesa Verde in Colorado, and Platt in the Territory of Oklahoma, 1906. The idea quickly spread to other nations. By 1920, there were sixteen parks in the United States, and parks were created in Argentina, Sweden, Switzerland, Canada, New Zealand, Australia, and Yugoslavia. The movement continued to spread until, by 1939, there were parks in Africa, Asia, Russia, and eastern Europe.

The existence of these preserves is credited with the saving of many wildlife species. Even today, game animals are trapped in national parks and moved to areas where the game has been extirpated. Many of the now-vigorous elk (wapiti) herds in the western United States, for instance, are descended from Yellowstone stock.

Governmental agencies were created or assigned to manage these new preserves, and many additional lands were set aside for wildlife. But wildlife management was still an embryonic science, and the agencies made many mistakes. Predators, long feared and hated for their occasional intrusions into human efforts, were destroyed by the thousand. This resulted in a tremendous increase of prey species, but because hunting was thought to contradict the purpose of a wildlife preserve in many cases, the animals were allowed to multiply. Yellowstone's elk became so numerous that, during the severe winter of 1919–20, more than 20,000 died. There were simply too many animals on the range. During the winter of 1961–62, trained park personnel killed more than 4,000 elk to bring the herd down to a level compatible with the range. Despite occasional grumblings from hunters, guides, and outfitters, park policy still does not allow hunting within Yellowstone's boundaries.

The elk controversy illustrates a basic tenet of conservation as we know it today. Nature operates in a balance as delicate as that of a fine Swiss watch. When man in all his ignorance pries it open and gropes about in its innards, discarding parts at will and damaging its fragile mechanisms, the whole machinery is thrown into disarray. Sometimes, it is so severely damaged that repair is impossible. But there is one major difference between a watch and an environment. Man can make a new watch; he can never replace a wrecked environment.

This lesson has been ignored in too many parts of the world. Even when it has once been learned, it may need to be re-learned when man, prompted by political motives, greed, or simple curiosity, decides to tinker with wildlife and its habitat.

A case in point is the introduction of animals into areas where they have never before been present. This has been going on during the past century at a feverish rate and has usually had tragic consequences. The few successful introductions, such as those of the ring-neck pheasant and the brown trout into North America, seem to receive more attention than the thick history book of out-and-out failures.

The carp, hailed as Europe's wonder fish by the United States government, has so successfully invaded the waters of North America that it has pushed aside valuable native game fish and destroyed much important waterfowl habitat. The proposed introduction into Britain and France of the coho salmon, for example, has caused anxieties about its effects.

The muskrat was introduced into Europe as a valuable fur-bearer, but in most European countries, these North American natives became

C Specially contructed bird-feeding shelters like this can help upland birds to survive a harsh winter, when the cold and the snow make it impossible for them to find food.
D Branches from deciduous trees, stuck in snow, provide winter fodder for small game, such as hare and rabbit.

A In an essentially undisturbed condition, the coniferous forests of northern Scandinavia would, and did, support populations of such animals and birds as *(1)* moose and wolf, *(2)* marten, and *(3)* capercaillie. The forest itself *(4)* had little or no deciduous growth, and its trees grew, aged, fell, and rotted in a centuries-long rhythm *(5)*. The first impact of man was borne by the predators—most of them desired for their furs—and as their numbers fell, conditions grew more and more favorable for an increase in the non-predator population. At present, however, only the moose is thriving, as it is far more adaptable than the marten or the capercaillie, which need primeval-forest conditions before they can flourish.

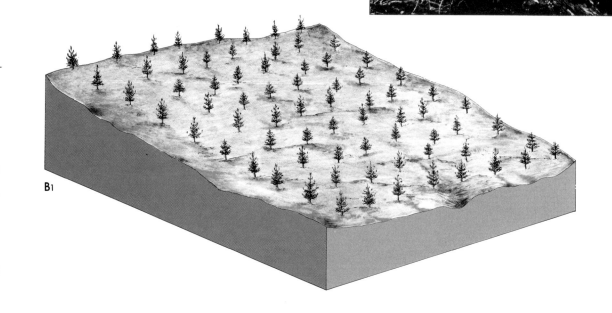

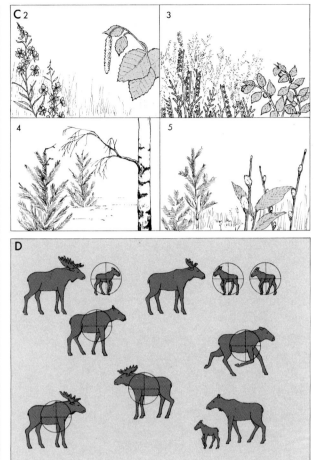

C1

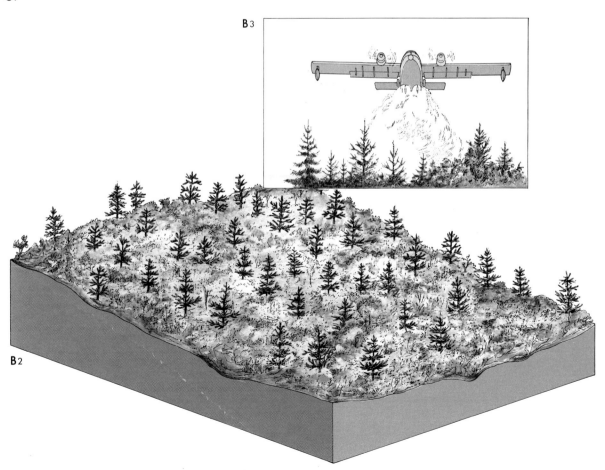

B3

B2

B The modern forestry industry's clear-cutting techniques remove all the trees in an area, and the land so cleared is replanted *(1)* with coniferous seedlings. After a few years, the young conifers are in danger of being crowded out by a rich growth *(2)* of deciduous vegetation—principally birch and aspen—which, together with certain young conifers, provides excellent food for moose. *(3)* Spraying with herbicide keeps the deciduous growth under control.

C *(1)* The moose thrives in the young pine plantations, where it eats the pine and deciduous plants. So great is the damage caused by moose to young pine in some areas that foresters are changing over to spruce, which the moose in those areas do not find so tasty. The moose's diet varies throughout the year: *(2)* in summer, it eats fireweed, willow herb, leaves, and grasses; *(3)* in fall, heather; *(4)* in winter, leaves, and shoots of pine and birch; *(5)* in spring, pine shoots and grasses.

D In the absence of the control once exercised by natural predators, the moose population in Sweden is culled annually by the carefully controlled shooting of a fixed number of bulls, cows, and calves. The numbers are based on census takings for each region.

45

A Finding out about an animal's habits, range, etc. is an important part of game management. Gathering information scientifically is made more easy by modern methods. *(1)* A wolverine is fitted with a collar bearing a radio transmitter. *(2)* The animal's whereabouts can now be plotted by means of a radio fix. *(3)* In winter, wolverines often run down and kill reindeer. *(4)* The wolverine's track. Although it cannot run fast, it has great stamina. *(5)* Its foot is relatively large and allows the animal to run on the surface of the snow, whereas the reindeer's hoof *(6)* plunges through the snow when it runs, and it soon becomes exhausted, falling prey to the wolverine.

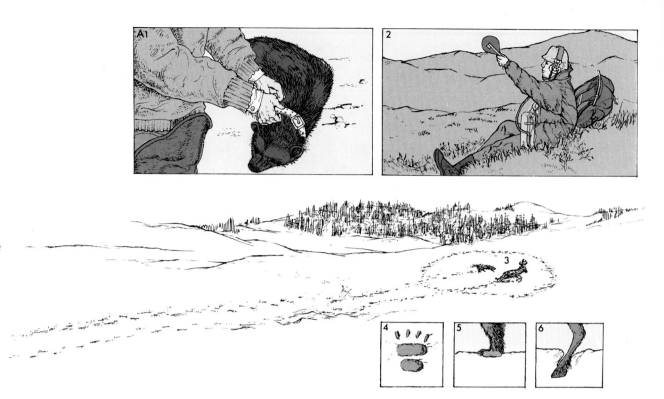

anything but valuable: they tunneled into railroad and bridge embankments, dikes, and ditches, and the authorities spent a fortune on trying in vain to destroy these pests. Another introduction from North America, less than a century ago, was that of the gray squirrel; at home, it occupied its own ecological slot, but it developed into a major pest in Britain.

The red deer, though a valuable game animal in Europe, became a pest in New Zealand after several were released there; so much so, in fact, that the government offered free ammunition to anyone who undertook to shoot one.

Mongoose were brought to Jamaica to control rats that were destroying the sugar cane. They controlled them nicely at first, but soon turned their predatory skills onto domestic poultry, land crabs, reptiles, and amphibians.

Yet the animal-moving trend continues. Coho salmon have been found in a Canadian stream that empties into the Atlantic, apparent escapees from a Maine fish farm. Some biologists fear that the cohos, which are natives of the Pacific coast, will compete with and drive out Atlantic salmon, which have been on the downswing for years. New Mexico and Texas are going full steam ahead with introductions of exotic big game, including oryx and Barbary sheep from Africa. Hungarian gray partridge are being hailed as the answer to declining pheasant hunting in the American Midwest.

Wildlife agencies, to be sure, are more careful with their policies than they have been many times in the past. Over much of the world, conservation is being practiced with wisdom and moderation. Wildlife management has developed into a respected, and often exact, science.

The work of the Game Conservancy in Britain is a leading example of organized investigation of game problems and restorative techniques. The Conservancy's experience has been drawn on not only in Britain but throughout Europe, including the Eastern Bloc, and in the Middle East. Game managers work in several ways, often building, but usually repairing damage to, wildlife populations. One of the most important of their functions is game research. Through it, biologists learn about the animals they want to manage and gain clues that aid them in making intelligent decisions. Such facts as reproductive potential, age and sex structure, food requirements, cover needs, and population trends are vital for the development of a smoothly working management plan. All these facts can indicate, for example, how much hunting can be sustained by a herd of gemsbok, the oryx of southern Africa, before its numbers fall drastically. A game manager needs a rough idea of what percentage of the animal population can be shot without ill effects on the herd as a whole. Then he develops a set of hunting regulations designed to allow an optimal harvest in order to persuade law-makers to set those regulations.

This is the point at which many perfectly good management plans are destroyed. Rule-making bodies often pay little attention to biological facts, preferring to regulate animal numbers for political or economic reasons. At times, law-makers decide that they are qualified to interpret biological findings and wildlife needs; so they set rules based upon their own false notions. This problem has been especially acute in North America.

Over the objections of wildlife biologists, several state legislatures in the United States have prohibited the hunting of female deer—a perfect example of how well-meaning law-makers can overrule politically powerless wildlife agencies. Habitat has been severely reduced during the past few centuries. Therefore, when doe killing is banned, the deer invariably multiply rapidly until the animals are too numerous for their range to support them in good health. Not only do deer starve, but the hungry animals damage their restricted range, sometimes so severely that dozens of years are needed for recovery.

In many parts of the world, agriculturists exert strong influence over game agencies, usually to demand more liberal game laws and, thus, fewer game animals to compete with livestock or to destroy crops. This is the case in much of Africa today and a major reason why elephant stocks

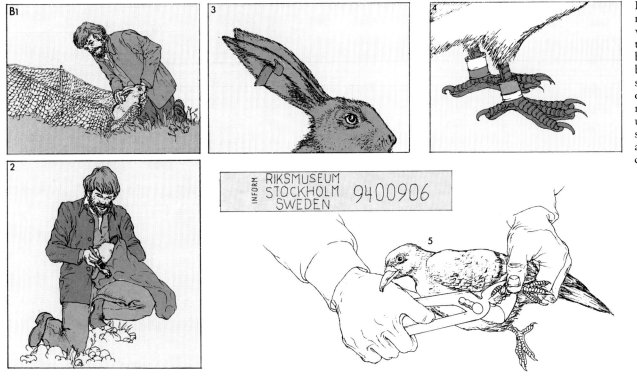

B *(1)* Hares are trapped in nets for marking. *(2)* This hare is being marked with paint on its leg. *(3)* This hare is tagged behind the ears. The tags will be invisible when the hare lays its ears back; predators will not be able to spot it too easily. *(4)* Birds are ringed on the leg with color-coded plastic rings. *(5)* Numbered rings are also used for marking birds. Hunters who shoot a tagged animal or bird should always mail the tags to whoever has carried out the marking.

are declining rapidly. The ponderous pachyderms are destroyed because their tree- and fence-crashing habits are incompatible with the needs of the ever-encroaching farms.

Properly used, however, hunting regulations can result in a maximum supply of game birds and mammals without allowing the resource to be degraded. Several species of ducks produce more juvenile males than juvenile females; yet the birds are seasonally monogamous—they mate with only one duck of the opposite sex. Thus, nature creates a surplus of male ducks—a surplus that can be harvested without resulting in a significant reduction of the next year's duck numbers. This is the underlying reason why hunters in certain areas are allowed to take more drakes than hens of particular species.

Preservation of key wildlife habitat is another game-management tool. How well man cares for and sets aside habitat today will determine to a large degree whether there will be sufficient wildlife to hunt in the future. Habitat preservation takes many forms: national parks, wildlife-management areas, wilderness-designated areas, government-financed leases of private lands, and private lands where development is prohibited by zoning laws. Some tracts of important wildlife land remain simply because they are unrewarding for cultivation or development. Builders frequently avoid flood plains and river bottoms, for instance. Farmers find their work too difficult on rocky, thin soils or on extremely steep slopes.

The tsetse fly, which carries the dreaded sleeping sickness in Africa, spreading it among livestock and humans, deserves credit for preserving many important game ranges. The tsetse has resisted control, and until recently, no vaccination against sleeping sickness existed. The invention of the new vaccine has worried some wildlife observers. If the tsetse is defeated, much game land will be opened to settlement, and some of the last remaining natural African wildlife areas will disappear.

Other important habitat seems secure. Some parts of the Rocky Mountains, for instance, particularly those drainages near population centers, are managed primarily as watersheds. To prevent soil erosion and loss of domestic water supplies, the government allows neither logging nor extensive livestock grazing.

Predator control is another management tool, but one that is not used as much today as it has been in the past. Only in the past few decades has the value of predators been accepted. Wolves, bears, wildcats, and other carnivores have been extirpated in much of the world, notably Europe and the eastern half of the United States. Now, efforts are under way to restore the predators—a plan that meets resistance from citizens who still regard wolves as nothing but cattle killers and bears as man killers. Such opposition notwithstanding, farsighted scientists in Europe are attempting to restock the European lynx into areas where it once existed. Mexico is working to raise the numbers of its native wolf, an endangered species. Just fifteen years ago, mountain lions and black bears were considered vermin in much of North America, but now they are classed as game animals practically everywhere they occur—except where numbers are too low to justify hunting.

Re-introduction of decimated wildlife, incidentally, is a relatively new, and extremely useful, tool of today's wildlife managers. It is used everywhere, from Asia to South America, but is most common in the United States, where the drug-dart was developed to immobilize animals. Biologists there are attempting to restore to former ranges several game mammals, including Rocky Mountain and desert bighorn sheep, pronghorn, and elk. Some mammals are moved to suitable habitat that, because of geographic barriers, never supported those species. Mountain goats have been introduced into the high mountains of Utah's Wasatch range and apparently are increasing. Moose were moved into Colorado in 1977, and reports are that the big deer are taking well to their new range.

Modern civilization is presenting wildlife biologists with new problems that demand solutions. In some parts of the world, road vehicles kill more game animals than hunters do. Conservationists have attacked this problem with enthusiasm but still have a long way to go. By charting road-kill reports, wildlife officers pinpoint trouble spots, and then erect

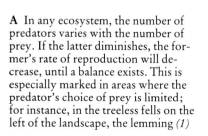

1

2

A

A In any ecosystem, the number of predators varies with the number of prey. If the latter diminishes, the former's rate of reproduction will decrease, until a balance exists. This is especially marked in areas where the predator's choice of prey is limited; for instance, in the treeless fells on the left of the landscape, the lemming *(1)* is one of the few sources of food available to the fox *(2)*. In a "lemming year," which occurs about every four years, these tiny rodents increase greatly in number. Shortly after, the number of fox cubs born rises sharply. If there is a shortage of lemmings, fewer fox cubs are born. On the lower ground, where the ecosystem consists of a greater number of elements, there are more prey species available, so the fox has a greater choice, and a more even supply of food, for instance field mice—a nest of young is shown *(3)*—rabbits, and ground-nesting birds; here, the variations in the number of cubs born annually is not so great as in the fells above the timberline.

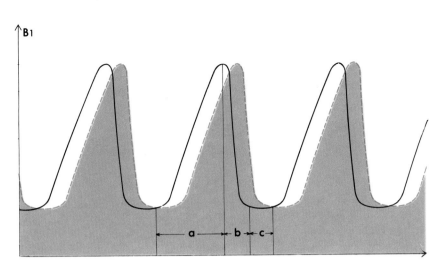

B1

B2

B The graph *(1)* shows that a similar relationship exists between *(2)* the snowshoe hare and the lynx. The vertical axis represents rate of increase and the horizontal axis represents time. During the years covered by time period *a*, when there is an abundance of food, the hares (their rate of increase is shown here as a whole line) multiply; shortly afterward, the lynx's rate of increase (dotted line) goes up. But as less and less food becomes available (period *b*), the hare's rate of increase goes down, until the population is at a minimum. Lynx numbers decrease, too, but not as rapidly, as the lynx can find alternative prey. During period *c*, growth is good, and there is more food for the hares, so their rate of increase goes up, although slowly at first, because the lynx help to slow down the rate. Later, they will not be able to stop it, and the cycle repeats itself.

A3

Every year, thousands of game animals are killed in road accidents, and the cost in human life and suffering is immeasurable. Many areas are now being fenced in, but when this is done, the game will not be able to pass freely from one area (which, perhaps, has become overcrowded) to another, so tunnels under the roads should be built.

signs warning motorists entering deer-crossing areas. In some instances, roadsides can be fenced to keep wildlife away from cars. But that is an expensive and frequently impractical solution. Fences also prevent game animals from migrating—a genuine threat to such creatures as pronghorns and caribou, which must roam over large areas to find sufficient food. Other attempts at reducing road kills have included reflective tape on roadside posts and large tunnels under the roads. The tape reflects the lights of oncoming automobiles, warning deer and other animals that danger is approaching. Tunnels have proved successful in some areas but have failed in others.

Feral dogs and cats are a problem around many populated areas, killing thousands of deer, pheasants, and other wildlife. Conservationists have fought this problem by encouraging laws that prohibit pet owners from allowing their pets to run loose and laws that promote birth control of pets. Most game departments encourage their employees—and often the public—to shoot feral dogs found chasing wildlife.

As game concentrates on the refuges man has set aside for it, the incidence of wildlife disease rises. This has forced wildlife scientists to learn to identify and fight these diseases. Unnatural concentrations of waterfowl frequently cause the birds to fall prey to such maladies as avian cholera and botulism. Though vaccines have been developed, inoculating large numbers of wild birds is out of the question. The solution is prevention, for once an epidemic strikes, thousands of birds can die within hours. To scatter large concentrations of birds, wildlife scientists have used aircraft, noise-making machines, and even hunters. The best method seems to be to eliminate one or more of the flocks' needs—primarily food or water. Often, the food that draws great numbers of waterfowl is man-produced—corn or other grain.

Some large ungulates can become infected with diseases borne by domestic animals. Brucellosis, for instance, can rush through and kill a herd of bison. Often, these large beasts can be trapped and vaccinated.

Other new immunizing techniques are also being tried. In parts of Europe, red foxes are the most common wild carriers of rabies. In an attempt to immunize the foxes, their most heavily used habitat areas are baited with pieces of chicken infused with an oral vaccine. If this experiment proves successful, the technique will surely be adopted in many regions. To reduce diseases among such animals as sheep, fodder laced with drugs is being used at some feeding stations. This is another experiment that seems promising.

But many types of wildlife cannot be given disease-preventing drugs, and so, many countries have passed laws strictly enforcing the examination and quarantining of imported domestic and wild animals.

Environmental pollution is a major conservation problem in modern countries. Though it probably affects game fish even more adversely and directly than game animals, its effects in many areas are extremely serious. Oil spills are bad and common enough, but the use of chemical cleaning agents along affected coastlines is probably no less harmful than the oil itself. One immediate effect of an oil spill is that a waterfowl's feathers, when soaked in oil, lose their insulation ability, and the bird dies unless it is rescued and cleaned. Pesticides and chemical defoliants, less visible but more threatening than oil, have directly killed thousands of birds and small mammals in some countries. The flora and fauna of Vietnam and Cambodia suffered immensely, not only from soldiers' guns, mines, and bombs, but from the defoliants used there to destroy enemy-hiding cover. Pesticides and other pollutants usually affect game animals indirectly. The young of most birds require the high protein found in insects, but areas heavily attacked with insecticides have few insects.

A major trend in game management today is toward intensive habitat manipulation. Ecologists have proved that most game animals prefer ecotones, which are edges between two distinctly different habitats—a forest and a meadow, for example. Ecotones often can be created by the use of fire, bulldozers, irrigation, seeding, or other methods. Such work is expensive and time-consuming but is often valuable, particularly when an increase in small game is the objective. Many of the most important wildlife refuges in the United States are controlled by systems of dikes and dams. By regulating the level of water, a refuge manager can create conditions suitable for the species he wants to increase. Certain kinds of ducks, for example, build their nests over two to three feet (1 m) of water. If the water is allowed to build to that level, those kinds of ducks generally raise their young successfully. Another use of regulating the water level is to control fish. When undesirable fish such as carp spawn in shallows, the water can be lowered to reduce the numbers after the eggs are scattered.

Fire control has only recently come into its own as a tool of wildlife managers, even though it was used by American Indians and has always been an important part of grouse management in Scotland. Many game animals, including most species of deer and upland game birds, are best suited to areas recovering from recent fires.

Fire prevention benefits the forest creatures but results in less habitat for animals that need brush, grass, or young forests. For many years, government agencies in the United States have routinely fought all wildfires, even those set naturally by lightning. Now the value of fire is being realized, though lumber companies and other special interests object strongly when fires are allowed to consume valuable lumber on large tracts.

Some densely settled forest areas cannot be allowed to burn because fire would endanger human lives or dwellings. To take the place of fire in the natural scheme of things, some wildlife authorities advocate clear-cutting. This has proved to be a valuable tool when done properly, but has resulted in the degradation of thousands of acres when not done in moderation or with proper concern for special conditions in the area.

Game departments throughout the world devote a large part of their resources to law enforcement. Without adequate enforcement, the best-laid set of wildlife regulations is next to worthless. Poaching is severe in many sections of the world, from the "civilized" states of the United States to the primitive bush in Africa. Certain game species face the threat of extermination from heavily poached areas. Rhinos of several types are threatened by poachers who kill for the horns, which are ground and sold as an aphrodisiac in Oriental countries. Elephant numbers have gone down drastically in recent years because poachers have killed the elephants only for their valuable ivory tusks.

The success of conservation depends in great measure on the attitudes and knowledge of the public. For this reason, conservationists on every continent are spending enormous sums on public education. In China, people are lectured on the value and importance of the giant panda. In Spain, attempts are made to persuade people that the brown bear, which lives in the remote mountains of the country and is essentially the same species that lives in North America, *Ursus arctos*, is worth saving. The developed countries publicize the dangers of pollution, clean-farming, and the rapidly skyrocketing human population, at the same time as they extol the values of wilderness preservation.

Of all the tools of the conservationist—whether he is a manager or a hunter—communication with the rest of mankind is probably the most important. If the world's wildlife is to survive the many threats directed toward it today, man must be convinced that the proper conservation of wildlife is essential to his very existence.

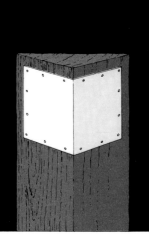

Less expensive methods of stopping game from wandering onto the roads include reflecting posts and markers. These reflect headlight beams and, hopefully, will scare off the animals, or at least make them wait until the vehicle has passed. One problem is that the reflecting surfaces have to be cleaned regularly.

Most road accidents involving moose occur during the summer months, as it is then that the previous year's calves leave the cows and begin to find their own way. Another bad period is in September and October, when the animals are in rut and are more or less unaware of any kind of impending danger. Dusk is the most dangerous time of the day, and it is then that most accidents occur.

Chapter 2
The Future of Game and Hunting

Richard F. LaRocco

One November day in 1976, two men—a 20-year-old automobile painter and a 71-year-old school custodian—experienced hunts that gave each an insight into the future of game and hunting. The younger man spent his day with his Brittany spaniel, hunting pheasants on his father's property along a muddy river. It was his last hunt there; the next spring, bulldozers would level the trees and brush, and fifty-three houses would be built. There would be no more room for the pheasants. The old man spent the day in a tree stand, a turkey permit stuffed in his pocket. He saw twenty turkeys and took a 13-lb (6 kg) gobbler. He was hunting on an abandoned farm in an area that had had no turkeys when he was a youngster. But farming there had become uneconomical during the years since his boyhood, and a hardwood forest now stretched over 350 acres (140 hectares) of once-cultivated farmland. Turkeys had been released there about five years earlier.

To the young man, hunting is an activity with no future. When he first started hunting at the age of twelve, pheasants had been common in the little valley where he lived. But soon, the valley became a suburb of a nearby city, and it was only on his father's farm that the last pheasants still persisted. Now, even it is gone.

To the old man, conservation has come a long way in the past fifty years. Not only are there turkeys on land that had none when he was a boy, but deer, grouse, and wood duck, all rare visitors once, have returned in number. Farming the steep, rocky ground is as unfeasible now as when the farm was abandoned, and the old hunter believes and hopes that the land will always provide food and shelter for game.

What *is* the future of hunting? Is there truly a place in tomorrow's world for wildlife? To answer these questions with any confidence, one would need a crystal ball; however, by studying past and current trends on the great hunting grounds of the world, one can get a fairly accurate idea of the direction things are taking.

What is inescapable will be the continuing effect of man's ecosystem on that of wildlife. The human population has grown fast over the past hundred years: from about 1 billion in 1850 to 2 billion in 1930, to 3 billion in 1960, to 4 billion in 1975. During this time, man's ecosystem has grown even faster, being enlarged by railways, motor vehicles, ocean, air, and space transportation, industrially constructed cities, and an industrially based agriculture. While only some parts of the world have had to absorb their combined direct impact in extreme forms, their indirect effects—their extractions and their refuse—has left, and will continue to leave, no part of the world untouched. And game and other animals thrive only when they do not trouble, or are not troubled by, any one of the parts of man's ecosystem.

Before about the middle of the nineteenth century, only a few parts of Europe and North America had been touched by the coming changes. In both these parts of the world there was—one can say with hindsight—perhaps the sense of a frontier. The limits of the untamed natural world had certainly been pushed back, and slow changes had been made to entire countrysides. For example, some 250 years of agricultural enclo-

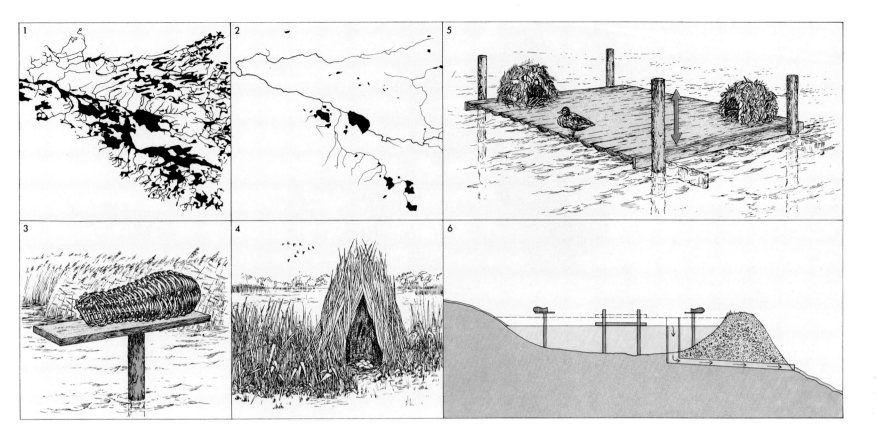

Excellent water-fowl breeding grounds like these are all too often subjected to draining, and this has a detrimental effect on the water-fowl population. *(1)* A water system with numerous connected expanses of water, interspersed with marshes and reedbeds. *(2)* If this is drained, the area changes character, and the breeding grounds that exist there will be destroyed. If a breeding population of birds is to return, it must have artificial nesting places *(3,4)*. Some nesting areas can float up and down as the water level changes *(5)*; in some places, a drain can be arranged *(6)*, so that flooding of the nests can be avoided.

The capture and release of wild turkeys. By this method, wild turkeys are transplanted from habitat with heavy populations of turkey to appropriate new areas that are unpopulated or only lightly populated. This increases the abundance and the distribution of the species, and in some cases, it saves whole turkey populations in areas where habitat will be reduced or disturbed by human activity. Several methods can be used for live trapping. The method shown here involves "cannon nets" *(1)*. A suitable clearing in a heavily populated habitat is baited with grain. At one edge of the clearing, a cannon with a large, light net is set up. When turkeys have gathered in the target area of the clearing, a concealed conservation officer fires the cannon, and the net shoots over the birds and traps them *(2)*. The turkeys are then transported in crates to the new area and released *(3)*.

sure in England had greatly changed the countryside's appearance and fauna. But even if some species were no longer to be seen in particular localities, and others—the dodo, the great auk, or the moa of New Zealand—had been made extinct, there must have been a sense that on the other side of the frontier, where man had certainly existed all the time, animals of all sorts still remained untouched in numbers that would have made our present fears incomprehensible.

It is largely with what still survives of those animals that hunters and conservationists are concerned today. But the demands of man's ecosystem are still increasing, and the role of the conservationist will be to moderate them if possible, and to make the best of them in any event.

What has the conservationist to contend with, then, and what means does he—or she—have available? The first part of the question is hardly difficult to answer: atmospheric, water-borne, chemical, heat, and noise pollution in all parts of the world; the increase in size and number of industrial activities, towns, and cities, and their domestic and industrial needs of land and water, in most parts of the world; mono-crop agriculture in North America, parts of Europe, Africa, and Asia; and the needs of rural populations in the poor countries for fuel and farming land. Within this worldwide context, conservationists have recourse to methods that are a mixture of the old and the new.

One of the persistent features of hunting for pleasure has been the protection of game in tracts of countryside reserved essentially for the use of the ruling classes, and the existence of laws providing fierce penalties for poaching. These conditions still obtain in many parts of the world, perhaps in their most developed form in Great Britain, where poaching laws have, however, been purged of their medieval barbarities. While England may be one of the most populated and industrialized countries in the world, and boasts royal game forests nearly 900 years old, it is unremarkable there that one person may own land, another may

farm it, a third may own the shooting rights, a fourth may lease the rights, while the local hunt may legally gallop across the land in the autumn, during the foxhunting season. All game animals, now including even deer, are owned by someone, even if it may sometimes be difficult to determine who that may be. Conservation is based firmly on the principle that shooting (and fishing) rights have a legal existence separate from that governing the land over which they are exercised, and can thus be bought, sold, and protected. Pollution, for example, or poaching thus infringes property rights.

Outside the reservations and the privately-owned hunting areas, conservationists must take account of the effects of agriculture on game animals and their food chains. That abandoned farm, where our 71-year-old hunted turkeys, had lost out, like tens of thousands of others, to industrial agriculture, a development of only the past three or four decades. Whole landscapes are now razed of hedges, fences, and ditches in the interests of highly sophisticated agricultural machinery that is used to process a single crop planted on an enormous scale. In Great Britain, some of the hedges that have been destroyed in this way dated back to the Middle Ages. In such a uniform environment, insect and plant pests endemic to the crop can spread explosively, so that they must be combated with chemicals on a large scale. Not only are birds and animals deprived of cover by the changes to the landscape, but their food is eliminated, while the residues of the chemicals inevitable affect water systems and harm the plant and animal life associated with them.

Industrial agriculture is perhaps more serious as a direct threat to wildlife, and a greater problem for conservationists, than industry itself, which is more concentrated spatially, and less direct in its effects. Agriculture and smaller game, at least, have always coexisted to some extent, for the damage done by such game was always to be balanced against the pleasure given by hunting it. There is little room for such

sentiments in industrial agriculture. Pesticide residues poison the fat of polar sea birds and animals, perhaps the most isolated of the world's creatures. Caribou and reindeer have high levels of radioactive strontium in their bones.

This is not to underestimate the effects of industrial pollution. Los Angeles, for example, has produced pollution that has killed or damaged an estimated 1.3 million ponderosa pine trees in the San Bernadino Mountains 75 miles (120 km) away. Animals depending on the trees for cover, food, or nesting have been reduced in number.

A vital part of intensive industrial agriculture is irrigation. It can cause streams and rivers almost to disappear, for rainfall is gathered up behind dams in reservoirs that themselves inundate valleys often richly stocked with game. When reservoir levels rise and fall in response to seasonal rainfall and take-offs, the shores cannot develop a stable waterside ecology, and it makes little difference from the hunter's point of view if the water is to be used for a hydroelectric plant, or for domestic or industrial use, or if it has been collected for flood control purposes. All of these instances, as well as large-scale drainage—something that has happened on a very large scale in Britain and mainland Europe—has caused riparian and other wetlands and their rich natural life to diminish. However, one cannot deny the positive side of man-made lakes. They can be stocked with fish and, gradually, an ecosystem that may be a novelty for the area is built up. Conservationists may feel themselves to be in a dilemma when this happens, for the introduction of exotic species is not always a good thing in the long run. Some extreme situations, however, require extreme solutions: power plants that pump out cooling water at a temperature of 80° to 90°F (27° to 32°C) have provided a new home for semi-tropical fish.

The introduction of exotic species is a process that has been going on at least since the Romans spread the pheasant over much of northwest Europe. Mistakes occur—taking rabbits to Australia is perhaps the best-known—but conservationists have seen brown trout and the ring-necked pheasant introduced successfully into North America, and many species there and elsewhere in the world have been preserved by planned re-introduction or establishment into areas where they once were, or could be made to feel, at home. Barbary sheep, for example, are now more numerous in the American Southwest than in their native North Africa, while Rocky Mountain goats have been successfully transplanted to the Wasatch Mountains of Utah. The "hot-holes" created by power-plant outflows have been stocked with such warm-water species as Florida-strain largemouth bass, tilapia, and hybrid striped bass, while birds that would otherwise migrate in winter remain all the year round and take advantage of waste grain in surrounding fields or of accessible aquatic plants.

Conservationists are directly concerned with such specific matters, and bring to bear an increasingly improved scientific knowledge of game and other animals in their ecosystems. They are concerned, too, with the implications for game of general industrial and agricultural pollution; nuclear power plants and their deliberate and accidental disposal of nuclear waste; the spread of suburbia in the industrial world, and that of farmlands and villages in the third world; the prospects of solar and wind-energy plants; and the overgrazing and exhaustion of farmlands, and the excessive clear-cutting of forests, with their attendant dangers of soil erosion.

Over-hunting has been a prime cause of the disappearance of many species and the near extinction of many more. Elk, whitetail deer, bison, and alligators are examples of species that have been saved at the last moment in the United States.

Improvements can flow from a better understanding of the role of predators in nature, to take one example, or from an appreciation that a

sentimental banning of the shooting or culling of does will lead to a rapid over-population that first severely damages the animals' environment and then leads to large numbers of deaths from starvation and disease. The effects of over-stocking of cattle—and therefore of over-grazing—are well known to conservationists. In the United States, the Bureau of Land Management, reporting on the rangelands of Nevada, stated that "uncontrolled, unregulated, unplanned livestock use is occurring on approximately eighty-five percent of the state and damage to wildlife habitat can be expressed only as extreme destruction." A similar situation surely exists in many other regions of the West and Midwest of America, while over-grazing in northern Africa is so severe that the Sahara Desert is moving southward. Over-grazing throughout the world has left depleted forage, damaged streams, and eroded soil. Too much stock has been competing for too long for too little food.

Knowledge has grown, too, of the importance of the controlled use of clearing and, even, of fire, in forest management. Wholesale felling has had, and continues to have, a major effect on animal life. This affected the eastern United States during the eighteenth and nineteenth centuries, affects India and Pakistan today, and has begun to affect parts of South America and Asia. Some species of deer thrive in the new growth that springs up after a fire, whereas a mature forest cannot provide this sort of grazing. Some game species, on the other hand—the turkey, for example—require mature forests. Too much felling, whether for game management purposes or to extract timber, can have far-reaching consequences if steep slopes are denuded of the vegetation that retains the soil. The dangers of such clear-cutting are both erosion and floods.

Today, game departments and conservation agencies are generally more cautious than they once were when introducing exotic animals. At one time, exotics were released into new habitats before their environmental needs had been evaluated and the possible effects of their new homes on their lives could be predicted. This resulted in a great number of failures or in "successes" in which the particular form of wildlife introduced became pests. Bighorn sheep from the north of the United States, for example, had been unsuccessfully reintroduced into a number of southern states before researchers pointed out that animals were needed that had adjusted to the climatic conditions they would meet in the South.

Hunters and conservationists find that their interests to some extent clash directly with those of the native peoples of the affected areas. North American Indians and Eskimos have had their claims to certain hunting and fishing rights upheld, in some cases by the Supreme Court of the United States, in others by local officials of either the United States or Canada. These rights include that of taking certain migratory waterfowl and their eggs in the spring. In northern Canada, this is, in fact, subsistence hunting, but now officials are seeking to give this right to all Canadian Indians.

In Africa and Asia, population growth has not only resulted in deforestation in the interests of farming and fuel, but has put pressure on game reserves. Rhinoceros are poached not just for their horns but for meat (and poaching for meat increases in the industrialized countries, too, as the price of fresh meat rises). Elephants cannot be physically confined in game reserves, and so are shot when they intrude on the villages and farms that are spreading all the time in Africa.

In some countries, the government reimburses farmers and ranchers for damage caused by wildlife. As the value of food continues to rise, such payments may cease. Instead, the game will probably be shot for "trespass." An alarming trend is the inclination of governments to increase game-damage payments. Often, as in some of the western American states, the funds for such payments come from fees charged to hunters and fishermen. Thus, money that could have gone to the improvement of wildlife habitat is going instead to farmers and ranchers.

When game damage is particularly high in some areas, the government sometimes buys the land outright and allows wildlife to feed on it. An alternative is to buy land nearby and lure wildlife on to it by providing

(Left) A herd of African cattle, still scrawny although the rains have begun, come home after a day's meager grazing. Too many cattle in proportion to the available growth progressively exhaust the grass, leading to soil erosion by winds and rain.
(Right) Deserts, and the arid and semi-arid areas around them, are growing all over the world. Trees are cut for fuel for the cooking fire or are destroyed by elephants; areas of shade, which retain moisture, shrink. Irrigation can cause the ground-water level to rise: as ground water is rich in mineral salts, over-irrigated land can become infertile and end up as desert.

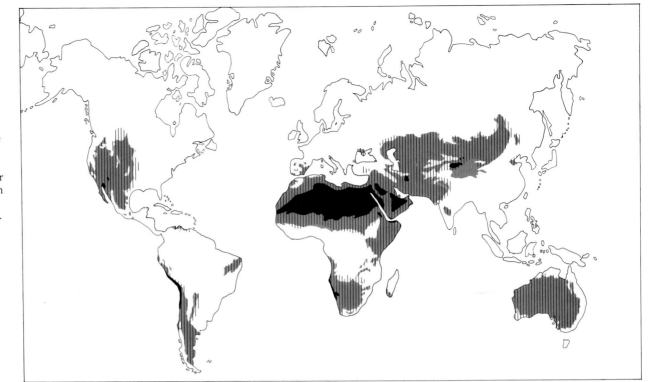

■ Extreme desert

▨ Arid

▥ At risk

food for the animals. Certainly, the costs of these programs will increase dramatically, perhaps to impossibly high levels. Obviously, there would be no necessity for game feeding if the animals had sufficient undisturbed habitat.

Another factor that increases the demands made on rangelands today is the growing need for more food. Nowadays, at least in parts of the world, the needs of wildlife are considered before range managers set livestock quotas. The question of livestock will surely receive even more consideration as the demand for more food increases. The problem is that many ranges can produce food only indirectly—by supporting wild and domestic animals. Since domestic animals can be controlled more closely than wild animals and are not subject to wide population fluctuations, raising livestock will be seen as the most efficient way to produce meat on the ranges. Wildlife will be destroyed or its needs ignored, if the demand for food becomes too great.

Sometimes, however, domestic cattle and game animals can occupy the same environment. In the United States, for example, the pronghorn antelope population has risen from about 13,000 at the turn of the century to some 400,000 today, despite the fact that some 2 million have been shot since the 1920s. This antelope has food and water requirements that differ subtly from those of the cattle that have replaced the buffalo on the Plains. While cattle can be fenced in by relatively light barbed wire fences—which pronghorn will not jump if they are more than about 30 inches (91 cm) high—the antelope can still wriggle under a lower, unbarbed strand of wire, if it is at least 16 inches (41 cm) above the ground, thus maintaining the freedom of movement that they need for survival.

In comparison to loss of habitat, other threats to game and to hunting seem inconsequential. The anti-hunting movement seems unimportant when possible events of the future are analyzed. But in the short term, at least in parts of the world, anti-hunting sentiment *is* a real threat to hunters. Preservationist groups in the United States have filed suits to stop hunts several times. In 1974, four groups went to federal court to challenge the United States Fish and Wildlife Service's waterfowl hunting regulations because of their lack of environmental-impact statements. Eventually, this suit was dropped. Then the preservationists sued again, this time in an effort to stop federal taxes on sporting goods from going to programs designed to benefit fish and wildlife.

In Switzerland, the Canton of Geneva actually put the matter of hunting to a vote, and hunting was banned for good. This kind of voting could spread, and that could mean trouble for hunters, who are a minority almost everywhere. Some cities in the United States have banned hunting on wide-open lands lying within city limits. This has been done mainly for emotional reasons, although safety is the usual pretext given.

Because whitetail deer were overpopulating the Great Swamp National Wildlife Refuge in New Jersey, state and federal officials called for a hunt in 1970, hoping to cull the herd to a safe level. Several anti-hunting groups intervened in court and successfully blocked the hunt that year and for three more years. In the spring of 1974, biologists searched the refuge and determined that about 60 deer had died of starvation because there was too little forage. Incredibly, the anti-hunters tried to stop the hunt again, but it was allowed in December, 1974. Autopsies on 63 of the 127 deer shot showed evidence of what had happened to the herd. One buck carried tumors weighing 7 lb (3 kg) on his head and was virtually blind because of them. Tumors of this kind had not been seen before 1974 and were not seen again after the hunt was finally allowed. Six-month-old deer killed inside the refuge weighed an average of 10 lb (4.5 kg) less than deer of the same age outside its boundaries.

Increased knowledge about predators and their role in nature is a definite improvement. Just fifteen years ago, bears and mountain lions were classified as vermin to be shot on sight in several western United States. Now, they are either fully protected species or game animals, and populations have increased dramatically. Idaho's black-bear population

(Above) A growing problem in conservation today is the huge amounts of oil that are being spilled into the ocean. Countless sea birds die every year, and the effect on marine life in many areas is disastrous. Once a bird gets a lot of oil on its feathers, they lose their water-repellant properties, and this leads to the bird's death from exposure, if it has not already been poisoned by the oil.

(Below) Biocides and the effluent from industry are today a serious threat to wildlife. For instance, it has been shown that, in the past thirty years, the shells of the merlin's eggs have become thinner, resulting in a high rate of death among chicks in the shell. Many eggs, as this one, are infertile. In the long run, the whole species will become weakened, if nothing is done about pollution.

has risen to such a high level that elk herds are suffering from bear predation on their calves. As a result, the state has liberalized bear-hunting regulations in some game-management units. In designated areas, non-residents may shoot two bears with a minimum of licensing formalities.

Perhaps the most promising trend, as far as hunters are concerned, is the increased public awareness of the environment. Laws designed to protect and restore natural environments have multiplied like mice in the past decade. Such laws are aimed not only at reducing pollution and other visible environmental degradation, but also at protecting vital wildlife habitat. The beneficiaries include a great many wild creatures, from rare and endangered species to game animals. Nowadays, wildlife needs often are given priority over such interests as those of livestock growers, miners, and developers.

Intelligent land-use planning has increased considerably. Some planners set aside areas for nesting and breeding grounds, winter big-game ranges, and flood plains, and prohibit development of such important wildlife lands for other uses. In Britain, duck populations have greatly increased since World War II thanks to inland conservation stimulated partly by the Wildfowlers Association (a hunting organization), and partly by private landowners cultivating duck as a replacement for the partridge, which has been reduced in numbers by mechanized farming methods.

Tourism is on the upswing in many areas, not only because some countries are getting richer, but because people have more leisure than ever before. Tourism rarely damages wildlife resources and often can be credited with saving them. The only hope Africa's wildlife may have is the tourist who will pay to see it or hunt it.

Hunters today support the official departments that are responsible for wildlife conservation more consistently and vigorously than they commonly did twenty-five years ago. Despite occasional disagreements, the public generally understands the need for certain regulations. The harvesting of female deer furnishes an important example. Traditionally, sportsmen have killed only antlered male deer—trophies—unless there was an unusual need for meat. Gradually and subtly, the trophy tradition acquired absurd overtones of chivalry: A gentleman must protect all females, even if those females happen to be deer rather than humans. Thus, sportsmen were quick to advocate and support laws against doe shooting, even though most of them were willing to harvest any buck, whether or not its antlers qualified as a trophy.

In regions where deer were scarce and habitat was adequate, protection of does was a good conservation tool; it permitted great increases in the herds. But the problem in those regions is no longer underpopulation. It is just the opposite—deer overpopulation.

Years ago, when game departments first suggested the harvesting of does as a form of population control, sportsmen were appalled, and for a long time, they continued to oppose doe harvests. Now, these sportsmen support the doe-control regulation, and many of them apply for doe permits, having come to understand that shooting does as well is the only way to curtail a deer overpopulation that eventually causes severe habitat damage and a massive mortality rate. In the past few years, several governments have held successful doe hunts for the first time in many years, simply because hunters were finally convinced of the necessity.

Concurrently, sportsmen are also attaining a new level of awareness with regard to ethical behavior. This is reflected in the literature they read. Some sporting magazines today refuse to print anything having to do with hunting inedible creatures. They place emphasis on the joy of pursuit rather than killing. The sharpened ethical awareness is also seen in hunters' behavioral crusades, or movements, such as SPORT (Sportsmen Policing Our Ranks Together), HOW (Help Our Wildlife), and Operation Game Thief, in which hunters are encouraged to report poachers and game hogs. Perhaps we cannot entirely rid ourselves of hunters who violate game laws and ethical codes, but such people are no longer regarded with amusement. They are detested.

Will there be hunting a century from now? Probably. But it is likely that hunting opportunities will decrease, disappearing entirely in some regions. What kind of hunting will exist for our great-great-grandchildren depends on what courses of action we take today.

Another example of the effects of pollution is found among the seals of the Baltic. Sterility among the females is disastrously high—as few as twenty percent of them are fertile. This has been shown to be the result of PCB. The change in the ecosystem that will occur should the seal die out will eventually mean a change in the conditions under which we ourselves live. Some biologists warn that, for every species that dies out, mankind is taking a step nearer its own destruction.

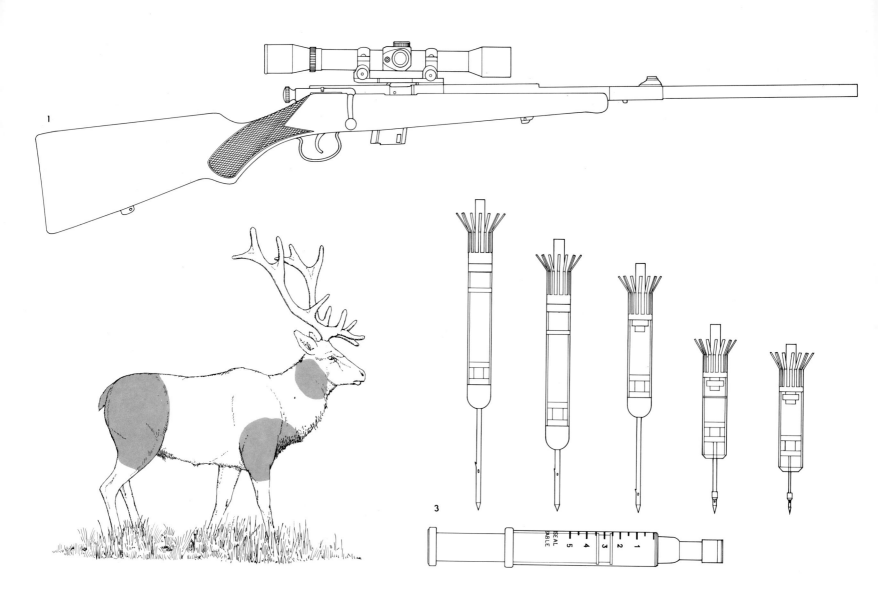

Tagging and radio-collaring various game species in order to monitor their activities and movements is an important part of game research. Often, it is important to be able to examine an animal (for instance, to take blood samples). For these purposes, some of the larger species are captured in baited pens; others are tranquilized or anaesthetized by means of a syringe projectile fired from a gun. Accurate marksmanship is a must when firing a syringe projectile at an animal. Drugs injected too close to the bone, in the joints between bones, or in tendons are more slowly absorbed than drugs injected in the muscle. The marksman should aim, therefore, at the animal's larger muscles in the rump, the fore-leg, or the hind leg (here shown shaded on a deer). Great care must be taken when choosing the optimum dosage, for this can vary for the same animal, depending on such factors as the animal's condition, the time of

day (if the animal has a full or empty stomach), and the weather conditions (if the animal is chilled, for instance, it will be less resistant to the drug). When using certain drugs, for example of the curare type, it is essential that an antidote be injected within eight minutes or so of the animal's collapse, as an immobilizing dose of this type of drug is capable of paralyzing the respiratory muscles, and this causes death in five to ten minutes.

The guns and syringes shown here have been developed especially for the purpose by Paxarms, a New Zealand firm. *(1)* The Paxarms Mark 20 Syringe rifle. *(2)* The Paxarms Mark 10 Smith & Wesson Syringe pistol. *(3)* A selection of syringe projectiles and a filling syringe.

III North America

Hunting laws and customs

Richard Comb

Two conflicting cultures shape attitudes toward hunting in the U.S. and, to a lesser degree, in Canada. On the one hand, many inhabitants of both countries are relatively few generations removed from a frontier society in which hunting was an important means of subsistence, and only one or two generations separate millions of people from a largely agrarian society in which wild game was a welcome supplement to the diet. North Americans take great pride in their frontier heritage and in the natural beauty of their land, and the passing on of hunting skills from one generation to the next remains for many people a happy and respected tradition.

At the other hand, North Americans are a rapidly growing and increasingly urbanized society. Outside Alaska, little true wilderness remains in the U.S., and much farmland has given way to development in the form of suburban housing developments, highways, office complexes, and shopping malls. Subsistence hunting has virtually disappeared. The result is a society in which increasing numbers of inhabitants have little contact with nature, and whose concepts of wildlife are formed largely by television and movies. Surveys continue to indicate that the majority of Americans are neutral on the subject of hunting, but there is no denying the growing influence of animal rights and anti-hunting groups. That influence is less noticeable in Canada, where vast tracts of wilderness remain intact and many inhabitants live closer to the land; nonetheless, Canada is not without its growing metropolitan centers, which exercise a disproportionate influence over political and cultural trends.

Offsetting the loss of wildlife habitat in the U.S. is the effective management of game and nongame species. Careful manipulation of remaining habitat to benefit wildlife, tracking of population trends of various species, and control of hunting seasons and bag limits have in recent decades greatly increased the population of some species, including whitetail deer, Canada geese, elk, and turkeys.

Habitat improvement is not restricted to public property. Various incentives have long been provided to encourage private land owners, particularly farmers, to engage in practices that prevent soil erosion and maintain an environment that is beneficial to plant and wildlife species, including game. Many state departments of conservation or wildlife work closely with cooperative landowners in promoting optimum populations of game and nongame wildlife. Many environmental or conservation organizations promote such activities. In addition, numerous private organizations exist whose primary purpose is to promote the management of a single species of game. Examples include the Ruffed Grouse Society, Quail Unlimited, Ducks Unlimited, Pheasants Forever, and the National Wild Turkey Federation. Though the focus of such organizations is on a single species, they are well aware that the conservation work they undertake benefits many species, including nongame animals.

Whether on private or public land, wildlife is publicly owned in North America, and the privilege of hunting is extended to all citizens. At the same time, private property rights are protected. Hunters must have permission to hunt on private property, and in many states that permission must be obtained in writing. Obtaining such permission is increasingly difficult in heavily populated areas. Much public land is available, and many tracts are designated specifically as wildlife management areas and are open to hunting.

Hunting regulations in both the U.S. and Canada are largely under the jurisdiction of state or provincial governments. Exceptions involve migratory species such as waterfowl, and special regulations pertaining to marine mammals, endangered species, and the interstate or international transportation of live or killed animals or animal parts.

Probably the most significant piece of federal legislation pertaining to hunting in the U.S. dates back to 1937 and the passage of the Pittman-Robertson Act. This act generates federal funds from taxes on the sale of sporting arms and ammunition and provides for the disbursement of these funds to the various states. Prior to the passage of the P-R act, many states diverted the revenues raised through the sale hunting licenses to purposes not associated with hunting. P-R funds are disbursed only to states that do not divert hunting license revenues to purposes not connected with hunting. Since P-R funds are substantial, such diversions are uncommon; the result has greatly benefited wildlife management in the U.S., as evidenced by increased populations of many species of game and nongame species of wildlife.

Planning a Hunting Trip

Careful planning, begun well in advance of the hunting trip, is the key to success. Properly done, the planning is an enjoyable prologue to the adventure of the hunt.

The first step will normally entail gathering information. For a wilderness big game hunt in Alaska, Canada, or the western U.S., planning should be undertaken at least one year in advance, preferably more. In a few cases, special permits must be applied for as much as six months prior to the hunting season; then too, many of the better guides and outfitters are booked solid a year or more in advance. For waterfowl or upland game hunting, planning six months in advance should be adequate.

A good place to start is with the wildlife departments of the states or provinces in which you are considering a hunt. These can provide information about seasons, bag limits, licenses and permits, and other regulations. Unless you are joining a local resident who will act as a guide, your chances of an enjoyable and successful hunt will be greatly increased by working with an outfitter, who can not only provide information but who can supply guides and necessary equipment. In some cases, outfitters or guides are required. Nonresidents hunting brown bears in Alaska, for instance, are required to hunt with a resident or employ the services of a licensed guide. In some Canadian provinces, all nonresident big-game hunters must employ a licensed guide or outfitter.

Booking agents are another option, and worth exploring. Booking an outing through such an agent does not add to the cost of the trip. If a hunter is in the earliest stages of planning a hunt, and the decision about where to hunt will be based exclusively on the quality of the hunting, booking agents can offer an advantage. A given outfitter may operate in one region, or even one location. A large, established booking agent, on the other hand, may have the option of arranging hunts with outfitters in a number of different areas. Established, successful booking agents have earned their success by working only with reliable outfitters.

You can usually acquire information about outfitters or guides from the states or provinces; another source of information about guides and outfitters exists in advertisements in hunting magazines. Sports Afield, Field & Stream, Outdoor Life, and Petersen's Hunting are among the more readily available such publications. If you are a bowhunter or a black powder hunter, there are publications directed specifically at these interests, and they will feature ads by outfitters or guides who specialize in these kinds of hunting. The North American Hunting Club, based in Minnetonka, Minnesota offers members a monthly hunting magazine and other services, including updated listings of outfitters and guides that have been recommended by members.

If you have a computer and access to the Internet, this can be a quick source of information. In many states, departments dealing with hunting are part of that state's department of natural resources. Executing a search using the key word "ODNR," for instance, will locate Ohio's Department of Natural Resources, revealing a menu that includes Ohio's Division of Wildlife, which in turn provides information about hunting seasons and regula- tions. The key word "WDNR" will turn up similar information about the state of Wisconsin, and so forth. Simply keying in the name of a state or province may provide leads to the agency that administers that area's wildlife and hunting. Key words including "hunting," "outfitters," "guides," and so on can turn up listings of hunting outfitters, and adding to those words the name of the region, state, or province in which you wish to hunt can narrow the search.

Another potentially valuable source of information is available on the Internet in the form of hunting forums. Soliciting information from hunters who live or have frequently hunted in the area that interests you can result in e-mail contacts who are happy to answer questions and help plan a hunt. The reliability of the sources is something to be evaluated carefully. Compu- Serve's hunting forum is among the oldest and best of such internet locations.

The information you gather will help shape the nature of the hunt you plan. At some point in your planning (the sooner the better) you will want to make some important decisions. For instance, if you are interested in hunting big game, you will want to decide if you are interested only in a trophy, or if you will be happy to fill your tag with any legal animal. Suppose you will be hunting elk, and are interested only in a trophy bull. Many hunters feel that the best, and generally most exciting, trophy elk hunting coincides with a period leading up to and including the peak of the rut, when bull elk respond to bugling. In many areas, this period (often in September) corresponds only with bow hunting. In some cases, a special primitive weapons seasons corresponds to the rut, and elk may be taken with muzzleloading rifles.

In a similar vein, white-tailed deer seasons are very long in many areas, beginning in early October in some states and running through January. However, this season may include periods restricted to bowhunting or hunting with muzzleloading rifles. The best chances for success on a trophy whitetail increase dramatically as the rut approaches. Throughout much of the U.S., the peak of the rut occurs near the middle of November. In the more northerly latitudes the rut may occur a little sooner, and in the extreme southern reaches of the country the rut may peak as late as December or even January. Modern firearms may be used during the rut in some areas, while in others only bows or muzzleloaders may be used during this period.

Other important decisions include the kind of environment in which you prefer to hunt, the physical demands of the hunt, the style of hunting practiced in a given area for a given species, and the kind of amenities you require for an enjoyable hunt.

Much excellent white-tailed deer hunting occurs in relatively densely populated agricultural areas. That is fine, unless you are planning a wilderness adventure. At the same time, if you prefer the amenities of civilization, do not want to spend a fair amount of time simply traveling to and from your destination, and do not want to spend the money required to enjoy the benefits of a first-class hunting lodge in the wilderness, you will find a midwestern, farm-country deer hunt better meets your expectations.

Most hunters will want to be sure that the hunt they are booking is a fair-chase hunt. The definition of "fair chase" may vary from one hunter to another, but as a general rule it is agreed that hunting animals in an enclosure is not fair-chase hunting. Some private preserves in the U.S. offer hunting for deer, wild boar, turkey, and exotic (non-native) species of game in enclosures as small as a few hundred acres or less. At the other extreme, some preserves enclose areas of several thousand acres or more. As you might expect, the hunting on these preserves, while offering relatively high rates of success, may closely approximate fair-chase hunting in many respects. It is also only fair to point out that some of these operations can offer hunters the option of hunting outside the enclosure for some species.

One indicator of whether or not a hunt is a fair-chase hunt is the guarantee such places offer. With few exceptions, outfitters cannot offer big game hunters a guarantee of success on a fair-chase hunt. A few outfitters offering fair-chase hunts do offer guarantees that a hunter will have a shot at legal game. The guarantee is considered fulfilled if a hunter opts to pass up a shot at any legal animal, or if he shoots and fails to harvest the animal. In some cases, the hunter is considered to have filled his tag if he wounds an animal that is not recovered.

Some forms of hunting in North America are physically demanding, and it is important that hunters be honest with themselves about the physical demands they are up to. Some elk hunting, for instance, as well as some deer hunting and most sheep hunting, takes place at high elevations. If you are not in excellent physical condition, and are not acclimated to higher elevations, your chances for success, not to mention enjoyment, plummet. It is a good idea, if you plan a hunt in the mountains, to arrive in the area a few days early in order to become acclimated before your hunt begins.

In the case of wilderness hunting, the means of transportation employed getting into and out of a hunting area can be an important consideration. Many Rocky Mountain outfitters pack into hunting areas on horseback. In some cases, hunters might be expected to pack in on foot. Small boats are used as a primary means of transportation in many parts of Canada. Some outfitters make use of planes, or even helicopters, to transport hunters to and from hunting areas.

Hunting methods vary greatly from one region to another, even for the same species. This is partly a matter of custom, but may also be influenced by local hunting regulations. For instance, bear hunting in parts of Eastern Canada and the U.S. is most commonly done by sitting in stands over bait. In most of these areas, dense vegetation and swamps make this the only practical approach to hunting bears. In other areas, hunting over bait is not legal.

Some states permit hunting bears with dogs. This is a physically demanding endeavor, and many hunters find it challenging and satisfying. Hunting with dogs is not legal in many states and provinces.

In areas featuring wideopen spaces, the typical approach to bear hunting is the glassand stalk method. In some of these areas, neither baithunting nor hunting with the aid of dogs is legal.

White-tailed deer can generally be hunted by a number of methods including stillhunting, sitting in treestands or ground blinds and, in a few instances, hunting over bait or with dogs. Some outfitters, though, specialize in one form of hunting or another, and might not permit hunting by other methods.

It is important to be clear about the kinds of amenities you expect on a hunt. At one end of the spectrum, hunters may stay in first class lodging providing many amenities and services. In the case of an unguided hunt, hunters are simply transported to an area (which may or may not feature a cabin or tent) and are on their own. In most cases, guides are expected to cook, clean up, skin game and prepare it for taxidermists or butchers, and generally provide for the safety and comfort of hunters. Guides are often available for each hunter, but hunters sometimes have the money-saving option of employing one guide for two or more hunters.

Another important consideration in planning a hunting adventure has to do with climate and special equipment needs. Most good outfitters provide lists of the equipment they provide, along with recommendations for personal gear the hunter should bring along. Climates range from extremely cold in the northern U.S. and Canada, to subtropical in the extreme southern U.S. Hunting in swampy areas, in either the North or South, may make rubber boots mandatory. Sun block can be important in the South. Insect repellent, depending on the season, can be important anywhere, especially in the wilderness. In the Southwest, and in some parts of the Southeast, hunters frequently wear high leather boots or chaps as protection against rattlesnakes. When hunting in the mountains or the western plains, a good pair of binoculars is considered an essential piece of equipment. Effective rain gear can be a matter of survival in the wilderness, and in many less remote areas can spell the difference between comfort and misery.

When it comes time to select an outfitter, a surprising number of hunters fail to ask for references. Any outfitter should cheerfully provide the names and phone numbers of references. Keep in mind that the outfitter is sure to select for references those clients who were happy with his services. Ask for the names of at least a few hunters who did not take game. Mistakes, oversights, and even some bad faith on the part of outfitters may be excused or even forgotten by hunters who filled their tags. Hunters who failed to take game are likely to provide a more complete and more candid evaluation of that outfitter's performance. If such a hunter can honestly say that he was happy with his experience and would not hesitate to book another hunt with the same outfitter, he has provided information that is probably more useful than that provided by successful hunters.

You may wish to ask questions about hunter success rates. Some outfitters are reluctant to provide this information; they feel, with some justification, that many outfitters inflate success ratios, and they do not want their accurate success rates to be compared with the inflated rates of other outfitters. Some also believe that it is inappropriate for hunters to attach too much significance to the kill, as opposed to the entire hunting experience. At the same time, success rates can be misleading. Do they reflect trophy animals or all game animals harvested? They normally do not distinguish between guided and unguided hunters, experienced hunters and novices. The pool from which the statistics are derived may include all persons possessing a license, some of whom never used it. The numbers also lump together hunters who hunted one or two days and hunters who worked hard for a week or more.

Nonetheless, it is not unreasonable for a hunter who is investing valuable time and money in a hunt to want some idea, however crude, of his chances for success. A few outfitters offering caribou hunts in Canada, for instance, claim success rates of over 100%. (The limit is two caribou per hunter in these areas.) In the state of Idaho, a recently published success rate for elk hunters was 6% In some cases, success rates are broken down to reveal differing rates for bowhunters, hunters using muzzle-loaders, and those hunting with modern firearms.

The needs of hunters vary greatly. It is important that a hunter feel comfortable with his outfitter or guide, and the level of comfort is usually determined by the quality of communications. Do not assume, however, that an outfitter will provide all essential information. In some cases, an otherwise excellent outfitter may assume knowledge or experience that a hunter does not possess. This is particularly true for hunters who are not residents of the U.S. or Canada. It is a good idea to have on hand a list of questions to present the outfitter. If the outfitter seems impatient with answering many questions, or if his responses seem evasive or incomplete, shop elsewhere.

Make certain you fully understand all the costs entailed in a hunt, and any additional fees that may be levied. There may be trophy fees for game harvested, for instance, that are added to the cost of the hunt. You may find that you have the option of bagging additional animals for a cost above that of the hunt you book. If you are hunting big game in a wilderness area, make sure the cost of getting the animal out of the wilderness is included in the hunt you book. Getting a moose out of a remote area may require an additional flight at an additional cost. Good outfitters should provide all this information up front, but reviewing all costs is always worthwhile.

Finally, some areas require that outfitters and guides be licensed, others do not. Whenever making use of a licensed guide or outfitter is an option, it is a good idea.

Hunting Waterfowl and Small Game

The U.S. features three major flyways for migrating waterfowl, including an Atlantic Flyway, a Central Flyway funneling birds down the Mississippi River, and a Pacific flyway. Waterfowl numbers, after declining for many years, appear to be on the rebound in North America. Excellent waterfowl hunting exists in many relatively heavily populated parts of the U.S., but some of the best waterfowling occurs in the northern plains of the U.S. and in the wilderness areas of Canada, with the Hudson Bay/James Bay area widely considered a waterfowlers paradise.

Much small game hunting, particularly for ringneck pheasants and quail, occurs in farm country. Grouse and ptarmigan hunting is excellent in more remote areas, and the plains of the western U.S. offer a bird hunter's smorgasbord of pheasant, quail, Hungarian partridge, prairie chickens, and other species.

The issue of fair chase is usually of less concern to small game hunters. Most upland game hunting in the U.S. is for wild game in its natural habitat (though, depending upon the species hunted, that habitat may include corn fields, wheat fields, or other agricultural crop lands). Hunters should be aware, though, that many shooting preserves raise pheasants and quail to be released for hunting, and some offer pass shooting at waterfowl that are released to fly to feeding areas. Hunters are placed at strategic locations to engage in pass shooting as the waterfowl fly over. In some instances wild bird populations are supplemented with released game to assure ample shooting opportunities. These practices are not so different from the kinds of driven pheasant hunts common in European countries. Still, if your expectation is that you will be hunting truly wild game in its natural habitat, such hunting would be disappointing.

Combination Hunts

Combination hunts for several species of big game are an option. In Alaska and parts of Canada, for instance, hunters may seek various combinations of caribou, moose, bear, wolf, deer and other big game animals in the course of a single hunt. Combinations involving big and small game are also an option. Chances of success increase, though, for hunters who concentrate on one or two species of game. Many hunters concentrate on big game, bringing along a shotgun for small game hunting should they meet with early success. Fishing, for those interested, is another option on some big game hunts.

These latter considerations can be important. The hunter who fills his tag on the first or second day of a hunt may be justifiably thrilled, but the elation could wear off quickly when the realization sets in that his long-anticipated hunt has come to a sudden end, and that a week or more of time remains before leaving. Many hunters can relish the opportunity to simply spend time in the area, observing wildlife, hiking, boating, or relaxing in camp. Most would enjoy more an opportunity to continue hunting for other species of big or small game or, for those so inclined, to fish.

Other Hunting Options

It could be that a hunter has planned a visit to the U.S. in the spring or summer. Though hunting options are limited during those seasons, they do exist.

Many states and provinces offer spring bear hunting--in fact some offer only spring bear hunting. Spring is an excellent time to hunt for bear, since they emerge from their winter hibernation hungry and on the prowl, actively seeking food. Bears are more likely during this period to travel during the day and to venture into the open. Spring bear hunting is very popular in most of the Canadian provinces.

An increasingly popular form of spring hunting in the U.S. exists in the form of turkey hunting. Wild turkeys were nearly exterminated in the U.S. around the turn of the last century, but thanks to aggressive management policies, populations are growing rapidly, and the wild turkey now resides in every state save Hawaii. Hunters pursue the male of the species, referred to as a gobbler or a tom. Spring is the mating season for the turkey, and the male engages in a mating call (a gobble) that reveals his location. He also engages in a courtship display involving fanning his tail, strutting, and emitting a mysterious, deep, humming sound called drumming. Hunting typically involves simulating the sounds of a turkey hen and thus bringing a gobbler into shotgun range. Wild turkeys are extremely wary and possess excellent vision, making them a challenging species to hunt. Chances for success are low for a novice hunting turkeys alone, but the services of an experienced guide can greatly boost the opportunity for a shot at this wary bird. The tails make for attractive trophies, and wild turkeys are excellent table fare.

Some species of North American game may be hunted year-round. Wild hog populations are on the increase in the U.S., and hunting them is becoming increasingly popular. In California, hog hunting is now the most popular form of the sport. It is also increasingly popular in the southern U.S. and in some Appalachian areas. Often considered a nuisance by farmers, in many areas there are no restrictions on hunting wild hogs.

Varmints of various species may be hunted year-round in many states. These include some predators, such as coyotes, foxes, and bobcats, as well as certain kinds of rodents including prairie dogs, woodchucks, and badgers. Varmint hunting can entail specialized techniques. Predators are often called into range at night, for instance, while prairie dogs or woodchucks are frequently shot at great distance with flat-shooting, high-velocity ammunition. Hunting regulations vary widely from state to state or province to province, with some areas offering unlimited hunting of some of these species, and others establishing closed seasons or bag limits, or requiring special permits.

Another possibility for off-season hunting exists in the form of Indian Reservations or properties. In some cases, Native Americans can establish their own hunting seasons and regulations for game on their properties. They may allow hunting for a fee, or may even offer package hunts that include lodging, meals, and guide services. Some of these advertise their operations in hunting magazines. State divisions of wildlife may also be able to provide information about hunting on reservations within their borders. The same caveats concerning booking hunts with outfit- ters in general apply equally to hunting on reservations.

Acquiring Licenses

Depending on the area and the species being hunted, hunters may be required to purchase some combination of licences and special tags and permits. This is not generally difficult, but can require advanced planning. Many licenses may be purchased over the counter at any sporting goods store, while others can only be purchased by mail from a division of wildlife. In some cases, special permits must be applied for well in advance of the hunting seasons, with deadlines occurring as early as June or July. Again, this information is available from the divisions of wildlife in most state or provinces. Any good outfitter should be able to provide this information, and many will make arrangements to provide all necessary licenses to hunters.

Application procedures vary. Hunters are sometimes required to send payment along with the application. As a general rule, payment is refunded if the application is unsuccessful. Application rules must be followed to the letter. There are a few important things to keep in mind. First, pay close attention to application deadlines. Make sure all requested information is provided. Some areas require different applications for different species of game, or even different areas within a state or province. Often, hunters are required to designate a specific hunting unit, with second or third choices should the first be unavailable.

Some hunts are quota or lottery hunts. Make sure you understand how these work. "Party permits" may be available for groups of hunters. This can sometimes increase the odds for successfully drawing to a lottery or quota hunt. In other cases, group permits may mean sacrificing the first choice of hunting unit. Finally, avoid applying twice for the same permit, since this may result in disqualification.

An increasing number of states and provinces require some form of hunter education course for hunters born after certain dates, the dates varying from state to state. Since most nations have more stringent requirements for hunters than do the U.S. and Canada, this is not a problem for the majority of hunters visiting North America. These requirements, though not stringent, are strictly enforced.

Planning an Unguided Hunt

Thus far we have assumed you will be enjoying the services of a booking agent, outfitter, or guide. The reason for this is simple: though it is certainly possible to enjoy a successful unguided hunt in North America, if you do not have experience hunting a given area, or do not have the luxury of experienced friends or relatives who can assist with such a hunt, your chances for unpleasant surprises are uncomfortably high.

Still, some hunters may wish to plan a do-it-yourself hunt, either because they find such a hunt more satisfying, or because such a hunt can be considerably more affordable. The key to success is extra diligence in planning and gathering information. All the information that would otherwise be available from out- fitters and guides must be obtained from other sources. You must provide your own gear, and make all your own travel arrangements. This in itself can be complicated; arriving in Alaska or the Canadian wilderness, for example, is only the starting point of your adventure. Vast distances may be involved in getting from an international airport to a designated hunting area, and for the most part the only way to get around is to charter flights into the bush. Various pitfalls await the inexperienced hunter. You might find that the gear you so carefully selected exceeds the weight limitations of small planes, to cite one example. Even a small detail such as a local prohibition of Sunday hunting can derail an otherwise enjoyable outing.

Certainly you will want good maps of the area you intend to hunt, including topographical maps. Canadian topo maps may be obtained from the Map Distribution Office, Department of Mines and Technical Services, Ottawa, Canada. If you plan to hunt in the U.S. in states east of the Mississippi River, maps can be obtained from the Map Information Office, U.S. Geological Survey, Washington, D.C. 20244. For western states, contact the Map Information Office, U.S. Geological Survey, Federal Center, Denver, Colorado 80225.

Finally, the previously mentioned hunting forums available on the Internet can be a real boon for the hunter planning an unguided hunt.

Visiting the U.S. and Canada

The special travel regulations and policies of concern to hunters include restrictions on firearms and hunting dogs, both in terms of bringing these into the country, and traveling between the two countries or within their borders. These regulations are subject to change, but currently are as follows.

Firearms may not be carried onto commercial aircraft (or many other forms of public transportation) or to the baggage screening points at airports. They may be checked as baggage, and must be contained, unloaded, in a hard case that is locked. When bags are checked, firearms must be declared. The baggage checker will normally ask that the case be unlocked and opened for inspection, and will place a firearms tag in the case, at which point the owner closes and locks the case and turns it over to the baggage checker. This process is not normally time-consuming, but not all agents are familiar with regulations. They may seek assistance from a supervisor, and this can be time consuming. Also, many airlines will not permit curbside checks of baggage. Allowing extra time for possible delays can help avoid the disaster of a missed flight. In both the U.S. and Canada, firearms must be registered with customs at the point of entry, and in Canada, visitors may be required by customs to provide the serial numbers and descriptions of any guns brought into the country.

Regulations on transporting firearms vary from state to state. The simplest and safest way to travel within the states, or between the U.S. and Canada by automobile, is to carry firearms unloaded in a case, and in the trunk of a car or the back of a truck when these options exist. Again, firearms must be declared at the point of entry when traveling between the countries.

Up to 1000 rounds of ammunition may be brought into the U.S. for sporting purposes. Any unused ammunition must be taken home when visitors depart. In Canada, the amount of ammunition that may be brought into the country is limited to 200 rounds.

Handguns are restricted in Canada, and may only be brought in under special circumstances requiring permission. In the U.S., handguns are legal for hunting in some states. Hunters must check the laws of the state in which they intend to hunt.

Dogs may be brought into the U.S. with proof of vaccination. The same applies to dogs brought into Canada, but a sixty-day quarantine period applies to all dogs except those brought in from the U.S., in which case proof of vaccination, signed by a veterinarian, is adequate.

Since these regulations are subject to change, hunters traveling to North America would be well advised to contact a Canadian or U.S. embassy or consulate before planning a hunt.

Hunting Customs

North Americans do not have the lengthy, comparatively formalized traditions belonging to hunters in other parts of the world, but they do attach great importance to their own codes of ethical hunting and rules of fair chase. These codes vary from region to region. Often hunting methods that are considered unsporting in one area may be the only practical means of hunting in another. Simple tradition is a factor, as well. In wilderness areas, where some kinds of hunting serve more to supplement the larder than to provide sport, codes of ethical conduct may be mitigated.

A few general rules apply almost universally, and some of these may be a matter of law as well as of ethics. First and perhaps most important, it is the ethical duty of every hunter to harvest game as humanely as possible. That means that hunters are expected to have some familiarity with their firearms or bows, and are expected to be reasonably good shots. They should know the effective killing range of their weapons, and should have some awareness of the caliber and load that is required to achieve a clean kill for whatever species of game they are hunting.

Every hunter is required to follow up on any animal fired upon. Only if he is certain of a clean miss can a hunter begin the pursuit of another animal. Otherwise, he must attempt to track the animal and make a diligent effort to recover it.

It is generally considered unsporting to fire on waterfowl that is on the water or ground, or upland birds that are on the ground, or any birds that are roosting, or any game animal that is in a nest, den, or burrow. (This does not include big game animals that are simply lying in the grass or on the ground.)

A few more caveats:

Unsafe handling of firearms is sure to earn the contempt of any hunting companions or guides.

Ethical hunters make every effort to avoid interfering with the pursuit of game by other hunters.

Ethical hunters always respect private property rights.

Given the range of traditions and hunting practices employed throughout the continent, visiting hunters should never hesitate to ask a guide or hunting companion any questions pertaining to these issues. Complex though hunting practices in North America may be, any visitor who enjoys hunting and treats guides, land owners, hunting companions, game, and the land that provides it with respect will likely find kindred spirits and be invited to return for another hunt.

IV Reference

Hunter's Lexicon

Jerome Knap
Wilson Stephens

Action: The breech mechanism of a gun, by means of which it is loaded and which secures the cartridge in the chamber, preventing the cartridge from discharging to the rear. Also, a field-trial term describing the manner in which a dog moves in the field; the British term is "style."

Afon: A stream in Wales.

Aperture Sight: See **Sights.**

Autoloader: See **Semiautomatic.**

Automatic: Any firearm which continues to fire, to the extent of the capacity of its magazine, so long as the trigger is depressed. Sometimes erroneously applied to semiautomatic firearms.

Automatic Safety: See **Safety.**

Backing: An expression of a dog's pointing instinct, when a dog comes to point at sight of another dog's point, to "back" him, or "honor" his point.

Balance: In theory, the balance is that point between butt and muzzle where a gun balances when rested on a fulcrum. A gun balances properly when the point of balance is midway between the points where the hands naturally hold the gun in shooting. However, this is not the common understanding of the term. In most cases, balance is understood to mean the feel it gives the shooter in handling the gun—that is, whether correctly balanced or either muzzle-light or muzzle-heavy.

Ballistics: The theory of the motion of projectiles. The shooter loosely considers "ballistics" to mean data relative to the velocity, energy, trajectory, and penetration of a cartridge, and sometimes to related factors such as chamber pressure and a powder's burning characteristics.

Barrens: Flat wasteland with low, stunted vegetation. Also, a broad, flat marsh.

Bay: Second point of antlers, after the brow and before the tray; sometimes spelt "bey."

Bead: See **Sights.**

Beat (n): An area to be beaten or driven to flush out game.

Beat (v): To beat bushes etc., to drive out game.

Beater (n): One who beats, in order to send the game over the shooters at a covert shoot or grouse drive.

Beck: A stream in northern England.

Bed: Where big game—or even hares or rabbits—have been sleeping or resting. Another term for a rabbit or hare bed is "form."

Belted Cartridge: A cartridge, primarily of the heavy-caliber, high-velocity type, which is rimless but has a belt around the base.

Belton: A type of color formed in English setters when two colors blend so closely as to lose individual identity. Blue belton is a combination of black and white; orange belton a combination of orange and white.

Bench Rest: A wooden shooting bench, heavily constructed and firmly placed, with suitable "rest" for the muzzle or barrel, at which the shooter may sit to engage in accuracy tests of the firearm.

Bevy: A group of game birds, such as quail, generally a brood.

Big-bore: A rather loose adjective, normally applied in North America to rifles of calibers larger than .25, but applied in some countries only to much larger calibers. Also, large-bore.

Blind: A natural or man-made hiding place from which a hunter shoots ducks, turkeys, or other game. The British term is "hide."

Block: Colloquial word for a duck decoy.

Blowback: Automatic or semiautomatic action in which extraction, ejection, and reloading are accomplished by means of the force exerted rearward by the gas of the fired cartridge.

Blowdown: A thick tangle of fallen trees and brush, usually the result of severe winds.

Blown Primer: A cartridge case in which the primer was blown out during firing. Can cause serious injury, even blindness, to the shooter; one good argument for use of shooting glasses.

Bluebird Weather: Sunny, windless conditions which are the bane of the wildfowler's existence, as waterfowl normally do not move in such weather or else fly very high.

Boat-tail Bullet: A bullet with a tapered rear end designed to obtain greater efficiency at longer ranges.

Bore: The inside of the barrel of a shotgun, rifle, revolver, or pistol, the diameter of which is the caliber or gauge of the weapon. The term is also a synonym for "gauge" of a shotgun.

Brace: Standard term for two quail, partidge, pheasant, grouse, hares, or dogs.

Breech: The base (as opposed to the muzzle) of a gun barrel; the rear portion of the barrel, which, in a modern rifle, is chambered to hold the cartridge.

Breeding: The ancestry of a dog.

Brocket: A male red deer in his third year.

Broken: Term for a finished, completely trained bird dog.

Brood: All young together born or hatched by one female. See **Bevy** and **Covey.**

Brow: The first, or brow, point of antlers.

Browse: Branches of trees, small saplings, or low brush, which serve as food for members of the deer family and other ruminants.

Brush-cutter: A bullet, usually of large caliber and considerable weight, having enough velocity and weight to continue its original course without being deflected by light brush.

Brush Gun: A rifle or shotgun with a barrel shorter than average, designed for ease of movement through heavy brush.

Buck: American term for the male of various species, including antelope, goat, deer, and rabbit; in Britain, of non-native deer imported to Britain, and of the rabbit. Also, an accessory used in teaching retrieving, sometimes called a retrieving dummy.

Buckshot: Large lead or alloy shot used in shotgun shells, principally for big game such as deer.

Buffer: A biological term used to designate small forms of animal life upon which predators will feed, thus reducing the mortality of game. When enough "buffers" are present, predators eat fewer game animals.

Bugle: The sound a bull elk (wapiti) makes during the rutting (breeding) season to advertise his presence to the females and to issue challenges to the other bulls. The British term is "roaring" for stags of European red deer. In some regions, "bugling" is also used to describe the cries of hounds.

Bump: Slang for accidental flushing of game birds by a pointing dog.

Burn: An area which has been burned over by a forest fire; also, a stream in Scotland.

Burst: Generally, the first part of the run when hounds are close upon the fox; any fast part of a chase.

Butt (1): The rear part of a gun stock from the grip area rearward.

Butt (2): Camouflaged embrasure in which a shooter waits for the birds at a grouse drive. Also, the backing behind a target that stops the bullets.

Butt Plate: The metal, plastic, or hard-rubber plate covering the rear of a gunstock, usually checkered or corrugated to prevent slipping. See **Recoil Pad** or **Stock**.

Calf: Young, either sex, of the red deer until a year old.

Caliber: The diameter of the bore of a rifled arm in hundredths of an inch or in millimeters, usually measured from land to land (raised portion between grooves), which gives the true diameter of the bore prior to the cutting of grooves.

Caller: A hunter who does the calling when hunting ducks, geese, or turkeys, or other game.

Cape: The hide or pelage covering the head, neck, and foreshoulders of a game animal, often removed for mounting as a trophy. The British term is headskin.

Carbine: A short-barreled rifle, normally much lighter in weight than a standard rifle.

Carrier: The mechanism in a magazine or repeating firearm (other than a revolver) which carries the shell or cartridge from the magazine into a position to be pushed into the chamber by the closing of the breechbolt.

Carry the Line: When hounds are following the scent, they are "carrying the line."

Cast: The spreading out, or reaching out, of a pointing dog in search of game or of hounds in search of a scent. Also, in archery, the speed with which the bow will throw an arrow. Also, in falconry, a group or flight of hawks.

Centerfire: A cartridge of which the primer is contained in a pocket in the center of the cartridge base.

Chalk: White excreta of a woodcock, indicating the presence of birds in a covert.

Chamber: The enlarged portion of the gun barrel at the breech, in which the cartridge fits when in position for firing.

Charge: Load of powder and/or shot in a shotshell, or the load of powder in a muzzle-loading gun. Also, an old command, still occasionally used, to a hunting dog to lie down; it derives from the time when gun dogs were required to lie down while the guns were charged.

Cheeper: Game bird too young to be shot.

Chilled Shot: Shot containing a greater percentage of antimony than soft lead. All shot except buckshot and steel shot is dropped from a tower. Buckshot of the large sizes is cast, as are single balls.

Choke: The constriction in the muzzle of a shotgun bore by means of which control is exerted upon the shot charge in order to throw its pellets into a definite area of predetermined concentration. Degree of choke is measured by the approximate percentage of pellets in a shot charge, which hit within a 30-inch circle at 40 yards. The following table gives the accepted percentages obtained with various chokes:

Full Choke..65 % minimum
Improved Modified.. 60–70 %
Modified .... 50–65 %
Improved Cylinder .... 35–50 %
Cylinder .... 25–35 %

Choke Constriction: The amount of constriction at the muzzle of various gauges, which produces choke, is as follows:

Gauge	Full Choke		Modified Choke		Improved Cylinder		Cylinder	
	inch	mm	inch	mm	inch	mm	inch	mm
10	.035	.889	.017	.432	.007	.178	0	0
12	.030	.762	.015	.381	.006	.152	0	0
16	.024	.610	.012	.305	.005	.127	0	0
20	.021	.533	.010	.254	.004	.102	0	0
28	.017	.432	.008	.203	.003	.076	0	0

Clip: Detachable magazine of a rifle or a pistol. A metal container designed to contain a given number of cartridges for a repeating rifle.

Cock (n): Male bird.

Cock (v): Make ready a firearm for firing by pulling back the hammer or firing pin to full cock. A firearm with a visible hammer usually has half-cock and full-cock positions.

Cold Line: The faint scent of the quarry.

Comb: The upper and forward edge of a gunstock against which the shooter rests his cheek.

Conseil International De La Chasse: An organization comprising members from various European countries, which assumes responsibility for the classification and measurement system employed in recording trophies of European big game.

Coon: A colloquialism for raccoon.

Cope: Muzzle for a ferret.

Couple: Two woodcock, snipe, waterfowl, shorebirds, or rabbits. Also used to describe two hounds.

Course: In fox hunting, to run by sight and not by nose. Also, the territory to be covered in a field trial for bird dogs and spaniels.

Cover: Trees, undergrowth, grass, or reeds in which game may lie. A place to be hunted.

Covert: In fox hunting, a place where fox may be found. Also, woodland. Also, the name for a place where any game may be found. Same as cover.

Covert-shoot: Pheasant shooting in which the shooters wait in line outside woodland from which the birds are driven by beaters.

Coverts: The wing feathers which cover the base of the flight feathers.

Covey: A group of game birds such as quail; a bevy. Also, a British term for a family group of grouse or partridge, generally four to sixteen birds.

Crimp: That portion of a cartridge case or shotshell, which is turned inward to grip the bullet or to hold the end wad in place, respectively.

Cripple: A game bird that has been shot down but not killed. This term is normally employed in duck shooting. (In upland shooting, the term "winged" is more often used.)

Cross Hairs: The cross-hair reticule or aiming device in a telescopic sight on a rifle. Wire or nylon is now used instead of hair.

Cry: The voice of a hound. The cry varies during the chase. By its tone, the other hounds can tell how strong the scent is and how sure the line is.

Dancing Ground: An area where such birds as prairie chicken, sharptail grouse, sage grouse, and black grouse perform their courtship dances in the spring.

Doe: Female of fallow, roe, or imported deer, and of the hare or rabbit.

Dogging: The shooting of grouse or partridges over pointers or setters.

Double: Any shotgun with two barrels, whether the side-by-side type or the over-and-under. Also, when a fox, raccoon, or other game animal turns back on his course to elude hounds.

Drag: Scent left by a fox as he returns to his den; or an artificial trail made by dragging a scented bag for hounds to follow.

Dram: Unit of weight, which is the equivalent of 27.5 grains. There are 256 drams in one pound avoirdupois (454 g).

Dram Equivalent: In the early days of black-powder shotshells, the powder charge was measured in drams. Dram for dram, today's smokeless powder is more powerful. The term "3 dram equivalent" means that the amount of smokeless powder used produces the same shot velocity as would 3 drams of black powder.

Drift: Deviation of any projectile, bullet, or arrow from the plane of its departure, caused by wind. Also, the deviation of the projectile from the plane of departure due to rotation. In all sporting firearms, the drift from the plane of departure due to rotation is so slight as to be of no consequence.

Drive (v): To move game toward the shooters.

Drive (n): A self-contained operation during a day's shooting in which the shooters remain stationary while game is driven from a particular direction.

Driven Game: Birds which are moved toward the shooters by beaters.

Driving: Method of hunting in which the hunters are divided into two groups. One group moves to an area to take up stands or watches covering a wide terrain; the other group moves toward the first, making sufficient noise to drive the game toward the group on watches. The individuals on watch are termed "standers" and those driving the game "drivers," or in Britain, "beaters."

Drop: Distance below the line of sight of a rifle or shotgun from an extension of this line to the comb and to the heel of the stock. See **Drop at Comb** and **Drop at Heel.**

Drop at Comb: Vertical distance between the prolonged line of sight and the point of the comb. The drop and thickness of the comb are the most important dimensions in the stock of a shotgun or rifle. They are affected by the drop at heel. If the dimensions are correct, the eye is guided into and held steadily in the line of aim. For hunting purposes, the best standard drop at comb on both rifles and shotguns is $1\frac{1}{4}$ to $1\frac{5}{8}$ inches (3.8–4.1 cm). Drop differs for target shooting. Ideal stock dimensions for field or target shooting are attained only by custom fitting.

Drop at Heel: The vertical distance between the prolonged line of sight and the heel of the butt. The amount of drop varies, depending upon the ideas and build of the shooter. Most shotgun hunters require a drop of about $2\frac{1}{4}$ inches (6.4 cm).

Earth: The hole of some burrowing animal, such as a woodchuck, appropriated by a fox. Also, the den.

Eclipse Plumage: The plumage of a male bird before the time when he takes on his full breeding plumage.

Ejector: Mechanism which ejects an empty case or loaded cartridge from a gun after it has been withdrawn, or partly withdrawn, from the chamber by the extractor. In a double-barreled shotgun, ejector often means extractor; "selective ejection" means automatic ejection of the fired shell only and is otherwise called automatic ejection.

Ejector Hammers: In a double-barreled shotgun, the driving pistons which eject the fired shells.

Elevation: The angle which the rear sight must be raised or lowered to compensate for the trajectory of the bullet and ensure the desired point of impact at different ranges.

Exotic: Any game bird or animal which has been imported.

Extractor: The hooked device which draws the cartridge out of the chamber when the breech mechanism is opened.

Fault: A check or interruption in a run by hounds caused by loss of scent.

Fawn: Offspring of the year of any deer other than red deer.

Field Dressing: The minimum dressing-out of a game animal in the field, merely enough to ensure preservation of the meat and the trophy, means usually the removing of the entrails and visceral organs.

Firing Pin: The pointed nose of the hammer of a firearm or the separate pin or plunger which, actuated by the hammer or the mainspring, dents the primer, thus firing the cartridge.

Firelighting: See **Jacklighting.**

Flag: The tail of a whitetail deer. Also, the long hair on a setter's tail.

Flat Trajectory: A term used to describe the low trajectory of high-velocity bullets which travel for a long distance over a flatter arc than other bullets. Scientifically an incorrect term, for no trajectory is truly flat. See also **Trajectory.**

Flighting: Ambushing duck or pigeon at their roosts or feeding grounds.

Fling: A period of aimless running before an enthusiastic bird dog settles to hunting.

Flush (n): The act of a questing dog putting game birds into the air, or an animal on foot.

Flushing Wild: Rise of game birds which have not been obviously disturbed, or birds that have been flushed out of shotgun range.

Flyway: Migration route of birds between breeding and wintering grounds. Also, the route waterfowl use between feeding and roosting areas.

Forearm: Synonymous with fore-end, although some use "forearm" when the butt stock and foregrip are separate pieces. See **Fore-end.**

Fore-end: Portion of the wooden gunstock forward of the receiver and under the barrel.

Forest: Open mountains, devoid of trees, on which stags are stalked in Scotland.

Fresh Line: Opposite of "cold line"— a fresh, or "hot," scent of game pursued by hounds.

Fur: All four-legged quarry.

Gaggle: A flock of geese. An old British term.

Game: In British law, pheasants, all partidges, all grouse, woodcock and snipe; by custom, also deer and hares.

Gang: A flock of brant. Also, an old British term for a group of European elk (moose).

Gas-operated: Said of a semiautomatic firearm which utilizes the gases generated by the powder combustion, before the bullet emerges from the muzzle, to operate a piston which extracts, ejects, and reloads the arm to the extent of the number of rounds in the magazine.

Gauge: The bore size of a shotgun. The number of the gauge has no relation to the linear measurement of the bore. Gauge is determined by the number of equal spheres, each of which exactly fits the barrel of the gun, which may be obtained from 1 lb (454 g) of lead. For example, a 12-gauge gun has a bore diameter the same as one of the twelve identically-sized spheres which can be made from a pound of lead. See **Bore.**

Gauge Measurements: The bore diameters of various gauges are as follows:

10 gauge	.775 inches (19 · 69 mm)
12 gauge	.725 inches (18 · 42 mm)
16 gauge	.662 inches (16 · 81 mm)
20 gauge	.615 inches (15 · 62 mm)
28 gauge	.550 inches (13 · 97 mm)
.410 gauge	.410 inches (10 · 41 mm)

Ghillie: Attendant, usually in charge of the pony, who accompanies a stalking party in Scotland. Also, an attendant on a fisherman.

Glass (v): To scan terrain with binoculars or telescope to locate game.

Grain: Abbreviated gr. Weight measurement. One ounce equals 437.5 gr. There are 7,000 gr in 1 lb (454 grams). In reference to gunstocks, grain indicates the direction of the fibers on the surface of the stock.

Gralloch (v): To field dress big-game animals immediately after shooting by removing the viscera and entrails. See **Field Dressing.**

Gram: Abbreviated g. Weight measurement. The equivalent of 15.43 grains.

Graze: Grasses, weeds, and similar low growths upon which deer and other ruminants feed.

Grip: That part of the stock of a rifle or shotgun which is grasped by the trigger hand when firing the gun. The two most common types of grips are the "pistol grip" and the "straight grip" found on some double-barreled shotguns.

Group: A series of shots fired at a target with a constant sight setting and point of aim. The diameter of the group is measured from the centers of the outer holes.

Group Diameter: The distance between centers of the two shots most widely separated in a group.

Gun: Any smooth-bore weapon projecting a charge of pellets; see also **Rifle**. Also, a participant in a British shooting party, as distinct from a helper or spectator.

Hair Trigger: A trigger requiring extremely light pressure for the release of the hammer.

Hammer: That part of a firearm, actuated by the mainspring and controlled by the trigger, which strikes either the cartridge rim or primer, or strikes and drives forward the firing pin so that it indents the primer or rim of the cartridge, to discharge the cartridge.

Hammerless: Of firearms having the hammer concealed within the breech mechanism.

Handgun: A firearm that is normally fired with one hand. A pistol or revolver.

Handloads: Cartridges loaded by hand for precision shooting, as opposed to commercial or "factory loads."

Hang-fire: Delayed ignition of the powder in a cartridge after the hammer has fallen and the primer has been struck.

Hard-mouthed: Of a dog that chews or crushes birds when retrieving.

Hart: The male deer. Usually used to refer to male red deer in Britain. A stag.

Head (n): The antlers of a deer, of any species and either sex.

Head (v): For a shooter to take post in advance of others to intercept birds flushing out of range of the rest.

Headspace: The space between the head of the bolt or breechblock and the base of the cartridge. Excessive headspace is exceedingly dangerous and can result in the bursting of the receiver.

Headstamp: The letters or number, or both, on the base of a cartridge.

Heel (n): Upper part of the butt of a shotgun or rifle. Also, a command to a dog to walk quietly beside or at the heel of the person giving the order.

Hide: Camouflaged embrasure in which a shooter waits for duck or pigeon. See **Blind**. Also, the skin of an animal.

High-base Shell: A shotgun shell furnished with high inside base wad, approximately ¾ inch (19 mm) thick before forming.

High-brass Shell: High-velocity shotgun shell on which the brass base extends a considerable distance up the plastic tube.

High Intensity: A term associated with a rifle or cartridge having a velocity of more than 2,500 foot-seconds (762 m/seconds).

High Power: A term associated with a rifle or cartridge having a velocity of more than 2,000 foot-seconds (609 m/seconds).

Hind: The female of the red deer.

Hochstand (Ger.): The seat at tree-top height from which deer are shot in woodland.

Hull: Empty cartridge or shell.

Hummle: A mature red deer stag which has grown no antlers.

Hunting: In British usage, the pursuit by a pack of hounds of ground quarry (fox, deer, hare) with followers mounted or on foot; gun sport is "shooting" in British idiom.

Imperial Bull: A bull elk (wapiti) that has seven points on each antler; a relatively rare and highly desirable trophy. Also, imperial stag in the case of European red deer.

Iron Sight: See **Sights**.

Jack: The male of the hare.

Jacklighting: The illegal practice of shooting game at night with the help of artificial light, which is reflected by the eyes of the game. Synonymous with firelighting.

Jump-shooting: A method of duck hunting in which the hunter stealthily approaches ducks by boat, or by stalking toward water, until within range and then flushes them.

Juvenile: A bird which, though having attained full growth, has not attained full adult characteristics or plumage. See also **Cheeper**.

Kentucky Windage: A term used by American riflemen to describe the process of "holding off" to the left or right of a target to allow for the effect of the wind on the bullet, but making no adjustment in the sight setting.

Knobber: Male red deer in his second year.

Lead (n): Term used to designate the distance it is necessary to hold ahead of any bird or animal to compensate for its speed of movement and the time required for the bullet or hot charge to reach it. The British term is forward allowance.

Lead (v): To cause a dog to follow under restraint, by means of a cord or leather thong attached to the dog's collar.

Leash: A group of three quail, partridge, pheasant, grouse, or hares. Also, a cord to lead a dog, a dog lead.

Length of Stock: The distance in a straight line from the center of the trigger to a point midway between the heel and toe of the buttplate, on the surface of the plate. Required stock length depends upon the build of the shooter, men of short stature or short arms requiring short stocks. The standard length for hunting arms is 14 inches (35.6 cm) for shotguns and 13½ inches (34.3 cm) for rifles. Also called length of pull.

Line: The track or trail of an animal indicated by the scent the hounds are following. Also, the shooters deployed at a formal shoot, called "the line."

Line of Sight: The straight line between the eye of the shooter and the target. See **Trajectory**.

Line-running: Of a dog that casts in straight lines rather than hunts in places where birds are usually found.

Line Shooting: A form of scoter (sea duck) shooting along the North American Atlantic coast, in which several boats line up across a known scoter flyway to shoot at the birds as they fly past.

Live Weight: The computed or estimated weight of a game animal before it is dressed out.

Loader: Attendant who holds and re-loads the second weapon when a shooter uses two guns at a covert shoot where many birds are expected.

Loch: A lake in Scotland (also lough (Ireland) and llyn (Wales).

Lock: The combination of hammer, firing pin, sear, mainspring, and trigger which serves to discharge the cartridge when the trigger is pulled.

Lock Time: The time elapsed between the release of the hammer by the sear and the impact of the firing pin on the primer. Also called lock speed.

Lubrication of Bullets: Most lead bullets have to be lubricated with grease or wax on their surface or in their grooves to prevent leading the bore. Outside-lubricated cartridges have the lubricant placed on the surface of the bullet outside the case. Inside-lubricated bullets have the lubricant in grooves or cannelures on the bullet where it is covered by the neck of the case.

Lug: In a break-down, breech-loading shotgun or rifle, a lug on the barrel secures the barrel to the frame. Lugs on the front of a bolt or breechblock which rotate into slots to lock the action for firing are termed locking lugs.

Magazine: The tube or box which holds cartridges or shells in reserve for mechanical insertion into the chamber of a repeating firearm.

Magazine Plug: Plug or dowel placed inside or against the magazine spring of a slide-action or semiautomatic shotgun to limit the capacity of the magazine in order to comply with the law. (In the United States, waterfowlers may have no more than three shells in their guns; some individual states limit magazine capacity for other game.)

Mark: A call used to warn another shooter of the flushing or approach of a game bird. The term is often accompanied by a direction: "mark right" or "mark left."

Mark Down: To use some terrain feature to mark the location of a fallen game bird in order to facilitate retrieving.

Market Gunner: One who hunted for the purpose of selling the game he killed, a practice now illegal in North America. A market hunter.

Mask: The head or pate of a fox, raccoon, wolf, or coyote.

Match Rifle: A rifle designed for competitive shooting, a target rifle.

Minute of Angle: This is the unit of adjustment on all telescopic, and most aperture, sights, being indicated by a series of fine lines. One minute of angle is equivalent to the following distances at the ranges indicated:

British and American	Metric
25 yards ......$\frac{1}{4}$in	25 m .... .69 mm
50 yards ......$\frac{1}{2}$in	50 m ....1.39 mm
100 yards 1in	100 m ....2.78 mm

Moor: High, treeless land such as that inhabited by grouse.

Mounts: Metal bases used to secure a telescopic sight to the barrel or receiver of a firearm.

Muzzle Brake: A device on the muzzle of a shotgun or rifle which, by means of vents and baffles, deflects gases to the rear to reduce recoil.

Muzzle Energy: The energy of a bullet or projectile on emerging from the muzzle of the firearm that discharges it. Usually designated in foot-pounds or kilogram-meters.

Muzzle Velocity: The speed of a bullet or projectile at the moment of emerging from the muzzle. Usually expressed in feet or meters per second.

O'Clock: A means of indicating a location on the target or over a range or field, corresponding to similar locations on the face of a clock, 12 o'clock being at the top of the target, or at the target end of the rifle range. Thus, a shot striking the target immediately to the left of the bull's-eye is a hit at 9 o'clock, and a wind blowing from the right at a right angle to the line of fire is a 3 o'clock wind.

Offhand: Shooting in a standing position, without the use of a rest or sling.

Over-and-under: Double-barreled firearm with one barrel superimposed over the other.

Palmated: Of the shape of the antlers of moose, caribou, and fallow deer that is similar to the shape of the palm of a hand with fingers outspread.

Pass-shooting: A form of shooting in which the hunter places himself in position under a known flyway or travel route of ducks, geese, pigeons, or doves. The birds are shot as they pass, without the enticement of decoys.

Pattern: The distribution of a charge of shot fired from a shotgun.

Pattern Control: Control of the shot pattern by means of choke.

Peep Sight: See **Sights.**

Peg: The numbered stick indicating the position of a shooter at a covert shoot or partridge drive.

Pelage: The fur, hair, or wool covering of a mammal.

Pellet: Round shot, of any size, a given number of which make up the shot charge.

Picker-up: One who, helped by dogs, finds and gathers what is shot.

Piece: The mid-day meal carried by a shooter.

Piston: In an automatic or semiautomatic arm, a metal plunger which, when forced down a cylinder by powder gases, operates a mechanism to extract and eject the fired cartridge, and to reload and cock the arm.

Pitch: This can be observed by resting a gun upright beside a wall with the butt or butt plate flat on the floor. If the barrel is exactly parallel with the wall, the gun is said to have no pitch. If the breech touches the wall and the barrel inclines away from it, the distance between the muzzle and the wall is the "negative pitch." If the barrel inclines toward the wall, so that there is a distance between the breech and the wall, this distance is what is called, simply, the "pitch." A pitch of 2 to 3 inches (5 to 8 cm) is desirable on a repeating rifle because it causes the butt to remain in place at the shoulder when the rifle is fired rapidly.

Point: The motionless pose assumed by a dog which indicates the proximity of game birds.

Points: The horn features of an antlered head which determine its ranking as a trophy (e.g. "a twelve-pointer" is brow, bay, tray, and three on top of each antler).

Point of Aim: The bottom edge of the bull's-eye for a target shooter using iron sights; the center of the bull's-eye for one using a telescopic sight.

Pointing Out: A method of shotgun shooting in which the shooter selects a point ahead of the moving target at which to shoot so that the shot charge and target will meet. Opposite shooting style to "swinging past."

Post Sight: See **Sights.**

Pot-hunter: One who hunts primarily for meat rather than sport.

Powder: The finely divided chemical mixture that supplies the power used in shotgun and metallic ammunition, technically propellant powder. When the powder is ignited by the flash of the priming composition it burns with a rapidly increasing gas which develops a pressure of 6,000 to 55,000 lb per square inch (420 to 3,900 kg per square cm) in the chamber and bore of the gun. This gas furnishes the propelling force of the bullet or charge of shot. Originally, all propellant powder was black powder formed in grains of varying size, with the size of the grain determining the rate of burning and suitability for various cartridges. Modern powders are smokeless and their base is nitroglycerine or nitrocellulose or a combination of both, the product then being called double-base powder. The rate of burning is controlled by the composition, by the size and shape of the grains, and whether or not coated with some retarding substance called a deterrent. Those so coated are called progressive-burning.

Primaries: The outer and longest flight feathers of a bird; quill feathers.

Primer: The small cup, or cap, seated in the center of the base of a centerfire cartridge and containing the igniting composition. When the primer is indented by the firing pin, the priming composition is crushed and detonates, thus igniting the charge of powder. Rimfire cartridges contain the priming composition within the folded rim of the case, where it is crushed in the same manner. The British term is cap.

Pull: The distance between the face of the trigger and the center of the butt of the gunstock. Also, the amount of pressure, in pounds, which must be applied to the trigger to cause the sear to disengage and permit the hammer to fall. Also, the command given to release a skeet or trap target.

Pump Gun: Common name for the slide-action rifle or shotgun. See **Slide Action.**

Quartering: A hunting-dog term for the act of ranging back and forth across the course.

Quartering Bird: A bird which approaches the shooter at an angle, either right or left.

Rat-tailed: Lacking long hairs on the tail, as in the case of such dogs as the Irish water spaniel.

Receiver: The frame of a rifle or shotgun including the breech, locking, and loading mechanism of the arm.

Receiver Sight: See **Sights.**

Recoil: The backward movement, or "kick," of the firearm caused by the discharge of the cartridge.

Recoil-operated: Of a firearm which utilizes the recoil, or rearward force exerted by the combustion of the powder, to operate the action and extract, eject, and reload to the extent of the number of rounds in the magazine.

Recoil Pad: A soft rubber pad on the butt of a firearm to soften its recoil.

Reduced Load: A cartridge loaded with a lighter than standard powder charge, for use at a short range.

Reticule (or **Reticle**): The crossed wires, picket, post, or other divisional system installed in a telescopic sight to permit its use as a gunsight, or in a pair of binoculars to permit the use of a scale for estimating distances.

Retrieving: Dog's act of finding and bringing an object, generally dead or wounded game bird, to the handler.

Revolver: Any handgun embodying a cylindrical magazine, as opposed to a single-shot or semiautomatic handgun, either of which is usually called a "pistol."

Rib: The raised bar or vane, usually slightly concave on its upper surface and usually matted, which forms the sighting plane extending from breech to muzzle of a gun. It is used on all double-barreled shotguns.

Rifle: A firearm projecting a single rotating bullet. Also, as the Rifle, the member of a stalking party who will fire the shot (cf. the Gun).

Rifled Slug: A bullet-shaped projectile with hollow base and rifled sides used in a shotgun for hunting big game. Will not harm shotgun barrels and will not "ream out" any type of choke.

Rifling: Parallel grooves cut into the bore of a rifle or pistol, spiraling from the breech to the muzzle, causing the bullet to spin in its flight.

Rig: A setting of decoys in front of a boat or blind; also used to describe the entire hunting outfit.

Rimfire: A cartridge in which the priming compound is contained in a rim at the base.

Ring Hunt: A form of driving in which a large number of shooters and beaters form a ring and gradually close in, to drive the game toward its center. An ancient method, still used in Europe, primarily for hunting hares and foxes.

Rough-shooting: The pursuit and taking of game and other quarry by Guns who have no human assistants but are generally aided by spaniels. See also **Dogging.**

Royal: Fourth point, after the tray and before the fifth, of antlers.

Royal Bull: A bull elk (wapiti) that has six points on each antler. A very desirable trophy. Also, royal stag of the European red deer.

Run: In some regions, a game trail or path created by animals over a period of time.

Safety: The device which locks a firearm against the possibility of discharge; sometimes called a safety catch. In common practice, the term applies primarily to the button, pin, or toggle which, when set in the "safe" position, prevents the discharge of the arm by pulling the trigger. A safety which automatically resets itself in the "safe" position when the gun is opened during the reloading process is called an automatic safety. Such a safety is most common on double-barreled shotguns.

Scapulars: The feathers on each side of the back of a bird's shoulders.

Scope: Telescope or telescopic sight.

Sear: The device in the lock of a firearm which holds the hammer or firing pin in its cocked position. When the trigger is pulled to the rear, it depresses the sear, which in turn releases the hammer or firing pin.

Secondaries: The wing feathers inside the primaries.

Semiautomatic: Any firearm which will fire, extract, eject, and reload by means of pressure on the trigger, but requires repeated pressure on the trigger to fire each round.

Set: A "rig" or setting of decoys.

Set Trigger: A trigger, the sear of which is "set up" by a preliminary movement or by pressure on another trigger, permitting the sear to disengage the hammer at the slightest touch or pressure on the trigger.

Most set triggers are adjustable for the amount of pressure desired.

Sewelling: Cords carrying colored streamers which, when activated, cause birds to flush far enough back to ensure that they are flying high when over the Guns.

Shell: Empty case of any cartridge. Also, an American term for a loaded shotgun cartridge.

Shock Collar: A collar with an electronic device which can be set off by remote control to give a dog an electric shock to punish it when it does not obey or does something wrong. The shock collar is a dangerous instrument in the hands of a novice trainer because it can ruin a dog when used incorrectly.

Side-by-side: A double-barreled shotgun with the barrels positioned side by side, as opposed to the over-and-under configuration.

Sight Radius: The distance between the front and rear sights. The longer the distance the greater the accuracy of the firearm.

Sights: The aiming device on a firearm. On most rifles and handguns, the factory-installed sights consist of two elements called "front sight" and "rear sight," which together frequently are called "iron sights" because they are made of principally metal. The front sight, located on the barrel near the muzzle, is usually post-shaped or bead-shaped and hence sometimes called post or bead. The rear sight is usually located partway down the barrel, near the breech or on the receiver. If it consists of a V- or U-shaped notch in a flat piece of metal, it is called an "open" sight. An open sight with a deep U-shaped notch with protruding wings is called a "buckhorn sight." The rear sight can also consist of an aperture in a disk. It is then called an aperture, or peep, sight. When the aperture sight is attached to the receiver it is called a "receiver sight" and when it is attached to the tang it is called a "tang sight." When the aperture adjustments have micrometer settings, such a sight is sometimes called a "micrometer sight." A hunting shotgun usually has only one sight consisting of a bead near the muzzle, but most trap and skeet guns have a second bead halfway down the barrel. There are also telescopic sights for rifles and handguns.

Sign: Any indication of the presence of game. Sign may include tracks, droppings, marks on trees, or any other indication that the area has recently been visited by a game animal.

Silvertip: Colloquial name for the grizzly bear.

Singing Ground: An open area used by the male woodcock for its courtship display.

Six o'Clock, or Six-o'Clock Hold: A term for the aiming point indicating that a rifle or handgun has been sighted-in to place the bullet not at the point of aim on a bull's-eye but well above it, so that the shooter aims at the center of the bottom edge. If the bull's-eye is a clock face, the point of aim is at 6 o'clock, but the impact point is at the exact center, midway between 6 and 12 o'clock. Target shooters prefer to aim in this way, when using iron sights, as it permits them to "rest" the bull's-eye on the top of the front sight and center the bull's-eye in the rear-sight aperture. See **O'Clock.**

Slide Action: A repeating firearm action in which the breech is closed and opened and the action operated by means of a sliding fore-end that acts as a handle for sliding the breech into the opened or closed position. Also **Pump Gun.**

Small-bore: Specifically, of a .22-caliber rifle chambered for a rimfire cartridge. Sometimes applied to rifles chambered for centerfire cartridges up to .25 caliber and shotguns under 20 gauge.

Smoked Sights: Sights after they have been blackened by soot from a candle or blackening lamp, thus eliminating any shine or glare. Commercial spray blackeners are also available.

Smoothbore: A firearm without rifling.

Sneakbox: A term for the Barnegat Bay duck-boat.

Spike-collar: A dog-training accessory—a slip collar with small spikes

Spook (v): To frighten game. A term used by a hunter to indicate that a bird or animal flushed or jumped from cover at his approach, or when it winded or heard him.

Spooky: Of any animal or bird that is extremely wary or constantly alert.

Spoor: Tracks or footprints of animals. Sometimes used to mean all game sign.

Spotting Scope: A telescope with sufficient magnification to permit a shooter to see bullet holes in a target at long range, and to permit hunters to see game and evaluate trophy animals at long range. The average sporting scope is 24 power.

Spread: The overall area of a shotgun pattern. Also, the inside distance between right and left antlers or horns at their widest separation or at the tips.

Spy: An interlude of halting, waiting, and watching in which a deer shooter observes his quarry and its movements before deciding the tactics of his approach.

Stag: The mature male of the red deer.

Stalker: The professional who guides and advises those seeking to shoot deer on open forests in Scotland; also, a shooter of deer in woodland who approaches the deer by stealth.

Stalking: A method of hunting in which the hunter locates game and then stealthily follows a predetermined route to arrive within shooting range of the quarry.

Stanch: Firm and decisive; describing a dog's style while pointing. The dog that establishes a point and holds it, without caution or admonition, until his handler flushes his birds, may be regarded as stanch. Also spelled "staunch."

Stand: The position at which the shooters are placed for each drive at a covert shoot (hence "first stand," "second stand," etc.).

Start: The moment when a hound first finds scent or a trail.

Steady: Of a dog's behavior after birds are flushed. The dog is "steady to wing and shot" when he retains his position after the birds are flushed and the shot is fired.

Still-hunt: A method of hunting in which a hunter moves very slowly and silently through cover in search of game, pausing frequently to scan the terrain. The word "still," in this context, means silent rather than motionless.

Stock (n): The wooden part of a shotgun or rifle, or the handle of a pistol or revolver. The butt section of a stock is called a buttstock.

Stock (v): In game management or preserve operation, to stock is to release game in suitable habitat.

Stop: An assistant tactically placed to prevent pheasants approaching the shooters too closely, or evading them, at a covert shoot.

Swinging Past: A method of shotgun shooting in which the target is overtaken and passed by the sight, and the swing with the target is continued as the trigger is pressed. See **Pointing Out.**

Switch: A mature male deer whose antlers have no points.

Take-down: Of a firearm in which the barrel and adjacent parts can be readily separated from the receiver or action, thus permitting the arm to be packed in a short container.

Tang Sight: See **Sights.**

Team: An old British term for a flock or group of ducks.

Telescopic Sight: A telescope with reticule, permitting an aim of greater accuracy and clearness than that of an ordinary sight.

Tertials: The wing feathers inside the secondaries that are closest to the body.

Throwing Off: Of a rifle that is performing erratically or failing to give reasonable accuracy. This often results from improper bedding of the barrel.

Timberline: The upper limit of forest growth at high altitude.

Toe: The lower part of the butt of a shotgun or rifle.

Tolling Dog: A dog once widely used in Europe, and used now only in Nova Scotia, to entice wildfowl to enter a trap or to lure them within range of the gun. The action of the dog in running back and forth on the shore stimulates the birds' curiosity. In Nova Scotia, these dogs are bred to resemble a red fox and are registered by the Canadian Kennel Club as the Nova Scotia tolling retriever.

Trade (v): Of game, to move back and forth over a given area: "The ducks were trading along the far shore."

Trailer: A dog which continually or frequently follows his bracemate.

Trailing: Act of following game. See **Tracking.**

Trajectory: The course described by a projectile in flight. It forms an arc due to the effect of gravity. Usually, measured in terms of height above the line of sight at midrange.

Tray: The third point of antlers of a deer, after the brow and bay (or bez). The word is sometimes spelt "trez."

Trigger Guard: A guard surrounding the trigger or triggers of a firearm.

Trigger Pull: The pressure required to bring about the release of the sear notch on the hammer, permitting the hammer to fall.

Tularemia: A virulent disease, known also as "rabbit fever." Rabbits are its major victims, and great care should be exercised when skinning rabbits. The disease can be communicated to humans if a cut or scratch on the hands or arms makes contact with an infected animal. The disease can be fatal. No harmful effects result from eating of an infected bird or animal, as thorough cooking destroys the virus.

Turkey Shoot: Originally, turkey shoots utilized a turkey as a target as well as a prize. The bird was placed behind a shield with only its head protruding. In early turkey shoots, contestants were permitted one shot in the standing position at 10 rods (55 yards/50 m); later, the ranges varied. At modern turkey shoots, a regulation target is used or clay targets are thrown from a trap, the turkey going to the shooter with the best score.

Turning to Whistle: A hunting-dog term for breaking the cast and turning the dog in response to the handler's whistle.

Twist: The angle or inclination of the rifling grooves off the axis of the bore. Twist is designated by measuring the number of turns or fractions of turns to the inch of barrel length. A "14-inch twist" means that the grooves make one complete turn inside the bore every 14 inches (35.6 cm).

Upland Game: A general term for all small game, including birds and mammals.

Various: In Britain, fair but unexpected quarry for which no category is provided in normal game records (e.g. jay, gray squirrel).

Varmint: A colloquial American term (stemming from "vermin") for a generally undesirable animal. Woodchucks and foxes are widely considered varmints. In some regions, the term is also used for predators such as bobcats. However, many predatory and non-predatory animals that were formerly classed as varmints are now protected or managed as game animals.

Varmint Cartridge: Cartridge designed to give exceptionally good accuracy, high retained velocity, and consequently flatter trajectory. Varmint cartridges are so called because they were originally developed for long-range shooting at woodchucks and prairie dogs.

Varminter: A rifle employed primarily for long-range varmint shooting. Many such rifles have long, heavy barrels for maximum velocity and accuracy.

Velocity: The speed of a bullet or shot charge, usually designated in feet per second or meters per second.

Velvet: Soft vascular tissue which covers the antlers of deer until they have attained their full growth and form, at which time membranous tissue dies and is removed when the animal rubs its antlers against brush and trees.

Ventilated Rib: A raised sighting plane affixed to a shotgun barrel by posts, allowing the passage of air to disperse the heat from the barrel which would otherwise distort the shooter's view of the target. Very useful on trap and skeet guns.

Vernier Sight: A rear sight, the aperture of which is raised or lowered by means of a threaded post with a knurled knob. A vernier scale on the frame indicates the elevation in hundredths of an inch.

Walk-up: A shooting method, chiefly for partridges and grouse, in which the shooters and their companions advance in line through a crop, stubble or heather, taking birds as they flush.

Wild Flush: The rise of game birds for no apparent reason, usually far from the gun.

Wing: All feathered quarry. See **Fur**.

Winged: A term indicating that a game bird has been hit but not killed. Used primarily by upland shooters. See **Cripple.**

Yard: An area, usually within a forest, in which a large number of deer, moose, elk, or similar mammals herd together, tramping down the snow and feeding on the browse supplied by the low branches. Used especially by whitetail deer when snow becomes deep enough to impede normal travel through browse areas.

Yaw: To vary from a straight course. A bullet which does not travel exactly "nose on" but wobbles slightly sideways is said to "yaw."

Yeld: A female deer without offspring; if a red hind, and barren, generally the leader of the herd.

Zero: The adjustment of the sights on a rifle to cause the bullet to strike a calculated impact point at a given range. A rifle with the sights zeroed for 100 yards will, under normal conditions, place the bullet in the center of the target at that range.

Bibliography

ACKLEY, P. O. **Home Gun Care & Repair.** Harrisburg, Pennsylvania, 1969.
ANDERSON, L. A. **How to Hunt Small American Game.** New York, 1969.
BAILLIE-GROHMAN, WILLIAM A. and BAILLIE-GROHMAN, F., eds. **Edward of Norwich: Oldest English Book on Hunting.** Repr. of ed. of 1909.
BARBER, JOEL D. **Wild Fowl Decoys.** New York, 1934.
BARNES, F. C. **Cartridges of the World.** Northfield, Illinois, 1972.
BERNSEN, PAUL S. **The North American Waterfowler.** Seattle, Washington, 1972.
BEST, G. A. and BLANC, F. E., eds. **Rowland Ward's Records of Big Game (Africa).** 15th ed. London, 1973.
BOUGHAN, ROLLA B. **Shotgun Ballistics for Hunters.** New York, 1965.
BOVILL, E. W. **The England of Nimrod and Surtees: 1815–1854.** London, 1959.
BRISTER, BOB. **Shotgunning: The Art and the Science.** Tulsa, Oklahoma, 1976.
BURK, BRUCE. **Game Bird Carving.** New York, 1972.
BUTLER, ALFRED J. **Sport in Classic Times.** Los Altos, California, 1975.
CAMP, RAYMOND R. **The Hunter's Encyclopedia.** Harrisburg, Pennsylvania, 1966.
CAPSTICK, PETER H. **Death in the Long Grass.** New York, 1978.
CARMICHEL, JIM. **The Modern Rifle.** Tulsa, Oklahoma, 1975.
CHURCHILL, ROBERT. **Churchill's Shotgun Book.** New York, 1955.
CONNETT, EUGENE V., III. **Duck Decoys.** Brattleboro, Vermont, 1953.
COYKENDALL, RALF. **Duck Decoys and How to Rig Them.** New York, 1955.
DALRYMPLE, BYRON. **Complete Guide to Hunting Across North America.** New York, 1970.
—**How to Call Wildlife.** New York, 1975.
DANIELSSON, BROR., ed. **William Twiti's the Art of Hunting.** Atlantic Highland, New Jersey.
DARTON, F. HARVEY. **From Surtees to Sassoon: Some English Contrasts 1838–1928.** Darby, Pennsylvania.
DA SILVA, S. NEWTON. **A Grande Fauna Selvagen de Angola.** Luanda, Angola, 1970.
DE HAAS, F. and AMBER, J. T., eds. **Bolt Action Rifles.** Northfield, Illinois, 1971.
DELACOUR, JEAN. **The Waterfowl of the World.** 4 vols. London, 1954–64.
DORST, JEAN. **Field Guide to the Larger Mammals of Africa.** London, 1970.
DUFFEY, D. M. **Bird Hunting Know-How.** Princeton, New Jersey, 1968.
—**Hunting Dog Know-How.** New York, 1972.
EDMAN, IRWIN., ed. **Socrates' Passages in Plato's "Dialogues."** New York, 1956.
ELLIOTT, CHARLES. **Care of Game Meat & Trophies.** New York, 1975.
ELMAN, ROBERT. **1001 Hunting Tips.** Tulsa, Oklahoma, 1978.
—**The Hunter's Field Guide.** New York, 1974.
ELMAN, ROBERT., ed. **All About Deer Hunting in America.** Tulsa, Oklahoma, 1976.
ELMAN, ROBERT and PEPER, GEORGE., eds. **Hunting America's Game Animals & Birds.** New York, 1975.
ERRINGTON, PAUL. **Of Men and Marshes.** Iowa City, Iowa, 1957.
FALK, JOHN R. **The Practical Hunter's Dog Book.** New York, 1971.
FITZ, GRANCEL. **How to Measure & Score Big-Game Trophies.** New York, 1977.

FORRESTER, REX and ILLINGWORTH, NEIL. **Hunting in New Zealand.** Wellington, New Zealand, 1967.
GATES, ELGIN T. **Trophy Hunter in Asia.** New York, 1971.
GREENER, W. W. **The Gun and Its Development.** London, 1881. Repr. 9th ed. New York, 1968.
GRESHAM, GRITS. **The Complete Wildfowler.** South Hackensack, New Jersey, 1973.
HALTENORTH T. and TRENSE W. **Das Grosswild der Erde und Seine Trophäen.** Munich, 1956.
HEILNER, VAN CAMPEN. **A Book of Duck Shooting.** New York, 1947.
HENDERSON, L. M. **Pocket Guide to Animal Tracks.** Harrisburg, Pennsylvania, 1968.
[HERBERT, W. H.] **Frank Forester's Field Sports of the United States.** New York, 1849.
HERNE, BRIAN. **Uganda Safaris.** Tulsa, Oklahoma, 1980.
HINMAN, BOB. **The Duck Hunter's Handbook.** Tulsa, Oklahoma, 1974.
HULL, DENISON B. **Hounds and Hunting in Ancient Greece.** Chicago, Illinois, 1964.
JOHNSGARD, PAUL A. **Waterfowl, Their Biology and Natural History.** Lincoln, Nebraska, 1968.
KNAP, JEROME. **Where to Fish & Hunt in North America: A Complete Sportsman's Guide.** Toronto, Canada.
KOLLER, L. **Shots at Whitetails.** New York, 1970.
KRIDER, JOHN. **Krider's Sporting Anecdotes.** Philadelphia, 1853.
MACKEY, WILLIAM J., Jr. **American Bird Decoys.** New York, 1965.
MARTIN, ALEXANDER C.; ZIM, HERBERT S.; and NELSON, ARNOLD L. **American Wildlife & Plants.** New York, 1951. MARTIN, ALEXANDER C., ed. Repr. ed. New York, 1961.
MELLON, JAMES et al. **African Hunter.** New York, 1975.
O'CONNOR, JACK. **The Art of Hunting Big Game in North America.** New York, 1977.
—**The Hunting Rifle.** Tulsa, Oklahoma, 1970.
—**Sheep and Sheep Hunting.** Tulsa, Oklahoma, 1974.
ORMOND, CLYDE. **Complete Book of Hunting.** New York, 1972.
ORTEGA Y GASSET, JOSÉ. **Meditations on Hunting.** New York, 1972.
OWEN, T. R. H. **Hunting Big Game with Gun and Camera.** London, 1960.
PETERSON, ROGER; MOUNTFORT, GUY; and HOLLOM, P. A. D. **A Field Guide to the Birds of Britain and Europe.** 3rd ed. London, 1974.
PETERSON, ROGER TORY. **A Field Guide to the Birds.** Boston, 1947.
—**A Field Guide to Western Birds.** Boston, 1969.
PETZAL, DAVID E., ed. **The Experts' Book of the Shooting Sports.** New York, 1972.
—**The Experts' Book of Upland Bird & Waterfowl Hunting.** New York, 1975.
REID, WILLIAM. **Arms Through the Ages.** New York, 1976.
REIGER, GEORGE. **Wings of Dawn.** New York, 1980.
RICE, F. P. and DAHL, J. I. **Game Bird Hunting.** New York, 1965.
ROURE, GEORGES. **Animaux Sauvages de Côte d'Ivoire.** Abidjan, Ivory Coast, 1962.
RUE, LEONARD L., III. **Sportsman's Guide to Game Animals.** New York, 1969.
SCOTT, PETER. **A Coloured Key to the Wildfowl of the World.** Slimbridge, England, 1957.
SPRUNT, A., IV and ZIM, H. S. **Pistols, A Modern Encyclopedia.** Harrisburg, Pennsylvania, 1961.
STEPHENS, WILSON. **The Guinness Guide to Field Sports.** London, 1978.
STEWART, J. and STEWART, D. R. M. "The Distribution of Some Large Mammals in Kenya." **Journal of the East African Natural History Society and Coryndon Museum** 24 (June 1963). Nairobi, Kenya.
SURTEES, R. S. **The Analysis of the Hunting Field.** New York, 1966.
TERRES, JOHN K. **Flashing Wings: The Drama of Bird Flight.** New York, 1968.
THOMAS, GOUGH. [GARWOOD, G. T.] **Gough Thomas's Gun Book.** New York
—**Gough Thomas's Second Gun Book.** New York 1972.
—**Shooting Facts & Fancies.** London, 1978.
TRENCH, CHARLES CHENEVIX. **The Desert's Dusty Face.** Edinburgh and London, 1964.
VILLENAVE, G. M. **La Chasse.** Paris, France.
WATERMAN, CHARLES F. **Hunting in America.** New York, 1973.
WELS, B. G. **Fell's Guide to Guns and How to Use Them.** New York, 1969.
WHITEHEAD, G. KENNETH. **Deer of the World.** New York, 1972.
WOLTERS, RICHARD A. **Water Dog.** New York, 1964.
WOOLNER, F. **Grouse and Grouse Hunting.** New York, 1970.
YOUNG, GORDON. **Tracks of an Intruder.** New York, 1970.

Index